SCENES FOR STUDENT ACTORS

VOLUME V

SCENES FOR STUDENT ACTORS

Dramatic Selections from New Plays

VOLUMES I, II, III, IV, V AND VI

EDITED WITH NOTES
BY
FRANCES COSGROVE

SCENES FOR STUDENT ACTORS

Dramatic Selections from New Plays

VOLUME V

EDITED WITH NOTES

BY

FRANCES COSGROVE

SAMUEL FRENCH

NEW YORK   LOS ANGELES

SAMUEL FRENCH (CANADA) Ltd. TORONTO

SAMUEL FRENCH Ltd.   LONDON

PREFACE

First of all, I must express my most profound thanks to those teachers and students throughout the country whose enthusiasm for these play cuttings has carried this series through the four preceding volumes, and now, brings it to the fifth. My appreciation is not entirely a personal something resulting from the success of these books. More than that, I think, is the very pleasant realization that only the ever-widening horizons of interest and achievement in the school theatre could bring about the successful reception of any book on theatre practice. It is with full consciousness of this notable advance in school theatre procedures that I have tried to fashion the contents of this latest volume of dramatic scenes for student use. I hope that both teachers and students will find them as useful as those in the preceding books in the series.

The selection of material for this volume has followed the pattern and policy which governed the compilation of the earlier books. Scenes are included which allow a wide variety of both solo and group work. A wide choice of both humorous and serious scenes by American and foreign authors is provided in forms that are both prose and poetry. As is usual in this series, all these scenes have the added motivation for student interest in that they are all taken from plays of contemporary interest because of the recency of their success in the professional theatre.

Even though this latest volume is the same as the others in both content and purpose, I am aware that in one respect it is different from the preceding collections. This one is to meet students and teachers who are working in a wartime theatre. Naturally aims, methods, and tastes will be influenced by the psychology of a nation faced with the job of winning a war. Undoubtedly some adjustments and compromises will be necessary. However, I am sure that most people of the theatre, whether professional or amateur, will realize that the main job is one of preserving the theatre intact, so that it may again take its high place in the culture of nations when peace comes again.

The authors of the plays represented in this volume and their publishers have been most kind in allowing me to reprint their work. To them and to Samuel French I offer my sincere thanks.

CONTENTS

vii

PAGE

The Cream in the Well—*dramatic* . . . Lynn Riggs 25

Gas Light (Angel Street) —*melodramatic* . . Patrick Hamilton . . . 26

FOR TWO WOMEN

The Lady Has a Heart—*comedy* . . . . . Ladislaus Bus-Fekete . . 29

Old Acquaintance—*comedy* . . . . . John Van Druten . . . 33

Spring Meeting—*comedy* M. H. Farrell and John Perry 34

Jupiter Laughs—*semi-serious* . . . . A. J. Cronin 37

June Mad—*semi-serious* . Florence Ryerson and Colin Clements 40

Morning's at Seven—*semi-serious* . . . . Paul Osborn 42

Mrs. Moonlight—*serious* Benn W. Levy 46

Eight o'Clock Tuesday—*dramatic* . . . . Robert Wallsten and Mignon G. Eberhart 47

FOR TWO MEN

One Mad Night—*comedy* James Reach 53

Abie's Irish Rose—*comedy* Anne Nichols 55

The Weak Link—*comedy* Allan Wood 57

March Hares—*satirical* . Harry Wagstaff Gribble . . 60

Good-Bye, Mr. Chips—*semi-serious* . . . . James Hilton and Barbara Burnham 62

Native Son—*serious* . . Paul Green and Richard Wright 64

CONTENTS

FOR ONE MAN

LOVE'S OLD SWEET SONG [1]

by

WILLIAM SAROYAN

The person who appears is a handsome man of fifty whose years are instantly irrelevant. He is, in fact, youth constant and unending. His hair is reddish, if not exactly red. His face is still the face of a young man who has better things to think about. He is wearing an old straw hat, and he is carrying a straw suitcase.

GAUL. You may remember, Ann, there were great troubles. There were panics in which a man rushed with the crowd to no place. No place at all. And I, with the million others, ran, and ran, forgetting love, forgetting everything but the need for escape. Protection from police and disease. Hideaways in fifty-cent rooms in large cities, in small villages. There were famines, Ann. . . . Hungry? Days, weeks, months, years of hunger. Hunger for bread, not love. Hunger for ease and comfort, not glory. There were disasters at sea. Shipwreck and storm. Floods and hurricanes, and a man off-balance falling in the street. Fear and shouting. No songs, Ann. There were distances, and barking dogs. Mountains to cross, and rivers and prairies and deserts. And wherever a man stood, his heart was not there. There was cold and few coats. There was ice and no fire. There was fury and stupor in the heart. As you dreamed here through the years, there was pain and forsakenness. There were accidents, Ann, with a man's body embarrassed by helpless and ugly posture, the arm twisted, the leg out of joint, and the heart in fever of disgust, raging against the mice. . . . Mice? . . . And the

3

foolish people asking, Are you hurt? Hurt? . . . I have been attacked by an army of termites as big as Japanese, and marching in the same military formation. There was snow and quiet, with the eyes of men staring out from secrecy and crime. There was hate, with the rain drenching the streets and the wind roaring around the buildings. . . . There were many things, Ann, to keep me away from you, as you dreamed here through the years. I remember the thirst I knew in Kansas City, and the bar-flies driving me mad. There were small things, Ann, insects and little words. Frowns and sneers. And big things. The stairway of the hotel on fire, and a man in his bare feet. There were moments, repeated a million times, that were useless to the years. And years that were meaningless to any moment. But I knew —always I knew, Ann—that you would not forget. I've come a long way, through many things, and still your face is bright. Your eyes still young. Your hand warm. Your lips soft and full. The errors that have been, I dismiss. Here, in your presence, I deny all I have known but good, since you are still by sweetness molded sweet. I here cease movement and begin dream, because here dream is real. And I've traveled across half the world. (*Solemnly.*) I'm tired, Ann. Now I must lie down in the sweet shade of love, and dream into the years of youth. The years of our youth, Ann. The years we have lost and shall now regain in the embrace of love.

DEAR OCTOPUS [1]

by

Dodie Smith

The Randolphs are having their annual Christmas reunion. NICHOLAS *is one of the more attractive members. He is talking with his Mother's secretary.*

[1] Copyright, 1938, by D. G. Smith. Copyright (Acting Edition), 1939, by D. G. Smith Beesley.

NICHOLAS. Do you know what I remember you in best? A grey flannel suit and a hat like a little pork pie. You wore it the first day you came here. . . . You stood there in the doorway, clutching a sort of gladstone bag—looking exactly like little Orphan Annie. . . . But seriously. Sit down a minute, I feel like talking. I was walking round the garden just now, looking at all the bedroom windows lighted up. There's something rather heart-breaking about family gatherings. . . . Oh, I dunno exactly. I suppose they make you realize the shortness of life—old age simply rushing at one. You know, once one stops being a child, time seems to get the bit between its teeth. Do you know, I'm nearly thirty-five? . . . But I've done nothing yet. . . . Advertising's interesting enough, especially now I'm a director. And I've a good many other irons in the fire. It's nothing to do with concrete success. I suppose it's some sort of spiritual lack. (*Moving to center of the sofa.*) Oh, hark at me! . . . Oh, I always get these broody fits when I come home. We used to be such a nice-looking lot of kids, and look at us now— Margery fat as a barrel, Hilda getting completely desiccated, and Cynthia sitting about registering the woman with a past. . . . Nothing grows old beautifully. Aunt Belle's a scream isn't she? Just held together with sticking-plaster. . . . Oh, the family, the family— I can never quite make up my mind whether I love it or loathe it. I believe I'd rather give fifty pounds than come to these gatherings of the clan. . . . They've got some sort of horrible fascination, even if they do start me thinking of death and worms. Do you know, when I was a kid, it used to infuriate me to think that this house— that any inanimate thing—could go on long after me. I say, why do you let me drivel on like this?

THE MALE ANIMAL [1]

by

JAMES THURBER AND ELLIOTT NUGENT

Ten years ago JOE FERGUSON *was a great all-American. He returns to the scene of his former glory—prosperous, dynamic, good-natured.*

JOE, *with coat off, is arranging plates, knives, saucers and forks on the floor in the form of a football formation.*

JOE. Now here—it's a balanced line. Move those two men out a little more. (PAT *moves the men out.*) This is a wonderful play! The coach gave it to me in the strictest confidence. . . . Now, study this play, girls, or you won't know it when you see it this afternoon. This is Michigan. And this is Midwestern. . . . Now! From the balanced line, we shift. Hup! (*He executes a Notre Dame shift, grimaces a little as his right knee resents this activity.*) Wally takes the left-end's place, but he plays out a little. . . . Michigan spreads out. They're watching that wide end, but it's too obvious. They're watching the other side of the line, too. . . . The ball is snapped back. Now look, here we go! Both of us. . . . (*Carrying a plate and a napkin.*) Close together. Fading back, but threatening a left-end run as well as a pass. . . . I'm both of them—Lindstrom and Wierasocka. . . . (*Comes forward.*) Skolsky cuts down the left side line deep and takes out Wupperman—that's the jam pot. (*He picks up "Wally."*) Wally is running wide around right end (*Runs around end.*) faking as though he had the ball but hasn't really got it—apparently! . . . Now, then, just as Michigan is charging in on Lindstrom and Wierasocka, trying to decide which one has the ball, Wally lets himself out! He's really got it! . . . It's a fake fake. It's an old play, so corny

only a football genius like Coach Sprague would use it.
With no interference at all, Wally cuts over and goes straight
down the right side of the field! He stiff-arms the safety
man. . . . (*Running with the cream pitcher.*) Touchdown!

BROTHER ORCHID [1]

by

Leo Brady

*The Florentine Brothers finding Little John Sarto of
Alcatraz in their petunia bed, severely wounded, nurse him
back to health. Using the Monastery as a hideout, Little
John joins the order choosing the name "ORCHID."*

orchid. That's kind of hard to answer. (*Almost turns away
in shame. He has never been sure when the sway of his orig-
inal motive for remaining lost its hold—he is not even sure
that it has—but, up to this, he had stopped thinking about
it. He scratches his head, takes a deep breath.*) I'll tell you.
When I landed here—in that petunia bed where you and
Lilac found me—natcherally I had no idea about sticking
around. I had other things to do. But I had to stay here a
while to heal up and there was something about it. I dunno,
it kinda got me. Where I was before, there was just a lotta
guys kicking and crabbing, see, and here I stumble on a
bunch of guys who is working their heads off for something
they believe in which is giving them nothing at all. At first
I don't believe it, and even after I believe it, I thought it was
a first-class whacky-house. Then I begin to think maybe
there's something to it, so I stay. . . . Well, now you take
these other outfits; they do a lot of book-writing and a lot of
talking. They get in touch with a lot of people that way. But
there's a lot of people they don't touch. Even these here mis-

sionaries who go to Africa don't get to a lot of people. They's
a lot of people, like—like me, see, who don't read books or
hear the preachers, see, and who have a tough time under-
standing them, anyway. Guys like that, it's the simple things
they know about, see, like you said—flowers and prayers and
being hungry. That's the things they think about and sometimes they see guys like—well, like Hollyhock, who is kind
of sissy about things and on account of them they throw over
the whole works. And even the guys that read the books,
well, books ain't everything, see, and that's where the prayers
come in, I guess, to help the guys who is too smart to think
about praying. And as for results, well, all you and me see,
maybe, is the garden and the dairy, but last week the Abbot
promised some money to help put on a new wing on the
orphan asylum. That's results, ain't it? Orphans has a tough
time, and they appreciate things like that, except (*And there
is a trace of autobiography in this.*) sometimes they're too
busy hating things, maybe, to think of it. I guess you got to
train people to get them used to kindness, huh? (GERANIUM
nods slowly.) Why, if the Floratines could bring one guy,
just one—to—to God, wouldn't that be doing something?
And I guess we can't be thinking about results all the time;
we got to just keep on working and hoping. Even if we don't
see the results, they must be there or the whole thing is a lot
of eyewash, ain't it? See?

GILLEAN [1]

by

CUMMING KENNEDY

GAVIN *is a fair-haired Irishman, gentle and composed. The
illness of his friend's wife recalls his own grief.*

[1] Copyright, 1937, by B. Cumming Kennedy. Copyright, 1940, by Samuel French.

GAVIN. Ay.
I like to think of her as I saw her first,—
A young slip of a girl—
In the little fishin' village in Argyll.
The sun was goin' down. She stood upon the rocks,
Her long hair blowin' out behind her there
Like brown seaweed in the curve of the wave,
And her great eyes fixed upon the out-goin' tide.
She was singin' to it.

She loved the sea with a passion that was surely strange.
Her father in his ancient Gaelic tongue would say
That from her birth the great pulse of the sea
Had beat in the veins of her,
And that she'd know no rest, no peace of soul,
Away from it.
A truer word was never said.—
For love of me she came out here
To the home that I'd prepared for her,
Out to the farflung prairies
Nigh a thousand miles from the nearest ocean bed.
In her years with me,
She never uttered a word of it.
But I knew . . .
Knew that her eyes were starvin' for the sight of it,
Knew that she was sick, sick for the sound of it—
For the boomin' beat of the breakers
On her homeland crags,
For the tappin' and the whisperin' of the spent tide
Seekin' her
On the shinin' cobbles
At her father's door. . . .
No word of her hunger ever passed her lips
Till that night she went,
Leavin' her helpless babe, but two days old,
Behind her.
All that night she was in high delirium—

Like our young Davie's mother, she was
"Talkin' strange"—
She had the smell of the seaweed in her nostrils,
She had the feel of the wet spume on her face.
I had my arm about her when she died.—
She sat up suddenly, her clear-brown eyes
Bright and gleamin' with the fever;
She clutched my hand, and she cried out, breathless-like,
"Can ye hear it, love, can ye hear it?
It's comin' in—the tide is comin' in!"—
Ay, the tide came in,
And the tide went out, takin' her with it—
Out of my arms . . . out of my life.

I HAVE BEEN HERE BEFORE [1]

by

J. B. PRIESTLEY

DR. GÖRTLER, *exiled from his own country, is living in London. A man of science and a philosopher, he has come to a small Inn in the Yorkshire hills to complete an experiment.*

DR. GÖRTLER. I lost my only son in the War—a young boy. I saw all my family and friends ruined by the economic collapse of Germany. I think it was the worry, the shame, of that period which killed my wife. And now I have seen my pupils taken away from me, and have been turned out of my university and out of my country. . . . Yet I do not hate life. I accept it all. Because, you see—there is no traitor—here— (*He touches his chest.*) . . . My wife used to say I remembered nothing. But that was because I always forgot anniversary days or what to take home from shops. (*He pauses and smiles across at* JANET.) It was peaceful up there.

. . . Every summer I used to walk on the Thuringian mountains—with my family and my friends. Ah!—we did not
even know how happy we were, to be together and have
such summer days— (*His voice drops; he is greatly moved.*)
I think it would have broken our hearts then to know how
happy and fortunate we were— . . . (*With an innocent natural pedagogic sense, half pathetic and half comic.*) These
high places have never been settled by men, so they are still
innocent. There is not about them any accumulation of evil.
Where men have lived a long time, the very stones are sat-
urated in evil memories. Cruelty and suffering remain in the
world, and I think the earth cries out under its load of evil.

THERE SHALL BE NO NIGHT [1]

by

ROBERT E. SHERWOOD

At Viipuri Bay DR. VALKONEN, *an eminent neurologist, de-
livers his last lecture in a little country school house. He has
been asked what difference "Whether men go to war because of illusion of glory, or just in a spirit of grim resignation."*

KAARO. There is all the difference. Because those illusions,
when shattered, leave men hollow. When men lose their illusions, they say, "Oh, what's the use? What have we got to
live for?" They are devitalized by the conviction of futility.
But grim resignation, as you call it, that makes a man say,
"This is an evil job—but I have to do it." And when men say
that, they are already beginning to ask, "But why do I have
to do it? Why must this evil go on forever?" And when men
start asking questions, they are not satisfied until they find
the answers. That is consciousness. And for the first time in

history, consciousness is not just the privilege of a few se-cluded philosophers. It is free for all. For the first time, in-dividual men are fighting to know themselves. . . . Forgive me, gentlemen. I forget myself. I think I am lecturing at the Medical Institute. But— (*He pauses to listen to the guns.*) —the Russians are only a short distance away. This may be my last lecture. So—please permit me to finish. . . . Listen! What you hear now—this terrible sound that fills the earth— it is the death rattle. One may say easily and dramatically that it is the death rattle of civilization. But—I choose to be-lieve differently. I believe it is the long deferred death rattle of the primordial beast. We have within ourselves the power to conquer bestiality, not with our muscles and our swords, but with the power of the light that is in our minds. What a thrilling challenge this is to all Science! To play its part in the ultimate triumph of evolution. To help speed the day when man becomes genuinely human, instead of the syn-thetic creature—part bogus angel, part actual brute—that he has imagined himself in the dark past—

THE TRIAL OF MARY DUGAN [1]

by

Bayard Veiller

JIMMY DUGAN, *a young and inexperienced lawyer, is de-fending his sister who is on trial for murder.*

DUGAN. Exception. (*There is a long pause.*) May it please the Court, Gentlemen of the Jury. (*He suddenly turns, and moves toward the footlights.*) I have been up all night lis-tening to the stenographer read the evidence in this case. It is pretty terrible, isn't it? Just how terrible it is to me, you cannot understand at this moment; but later you will. After I'd heard the appalling testimony against my sister, I talked with her. She hasn't any idea who killed Edgar Rice—neither have I. When questioned by the police, she was quite frank. She told them everything that she could tell them. One thing she did keep a secret from them. The identity of this mysterious Jimmy, about whom she spoke so often. This mysterious person who wrote to her so often—and whose letters meant so much to her. I am quite sure the district attorney is terribly disappointed in finding that the mysterious Jimmy was only the girl's brother. So, you see, it wasn't a lover after all that she cried over. Only a younger brother. And she will tell you herself why his letters meant so much to her. Why she cried over them— I know that when I heard all the evidence, bit by bit, piled up so eloquently and admirably by the District Attorney, I felt that there was no way out. What defense could I bring forward? My sister has no witness—I have no witness—I have only a certainty in my own heart that my sister didn't do this terrible thing. The fact of a blind faith and a great love isn't evidence. Is it? You will recall that each of the long line of witnesses who were sworn took the oath as follows: The clerk said to them—a little hurriedly, perhaps—"You solemnly swear to tell the truth the whole truth; and nothing but the truth." I think most of the witnesses—I will go further—all but one of the witnesses told the truth and nothing but the truth; but I don't believe that many of them told the whole truth. And this is what we want isn't it?—the whole truth. (*Crosses to chair.*) I have been advised by a brilliant lawyer of this city that the cleverest thing Mr. West did in his conduct of this case was to waive the cross-examination of Mrs. Gertrude Rice. He said to me, "My boy, that woman has the sympathy of the jury—if you put that woman on the stand, handle her with gloves." (*Crosses down center. He stops and holds out his hands toward the audience.*) Gentlemen, I have no gloves. I said a moment ago I wanted the truth. I'm going even further than that. I want you to have the truth. I want to put before you every fact in this case and I tell you with perfect frankness that at the present time I have no defense for my sister. No

defense beyond her bare word. (*Back of chair.*) Now gentlemen, I can see but one way to prove her innocence and that
is to fasten the guilt of this murder where it really belongs.
I don't know where that is. I don't know who killed Edgar
Rice—but let us bring these witnesses back again; let us go
a little deeper and let us see, gentlemen, if between us we
cannot discover who really did this thing.

NATIVE SON [1]

by

Paul Green and Richard Wright

In an abandoned house in Chicago, bigger thomas *is hid-
ing from the police.*

*Presently he turns and begins to pace up and down, beat-
ing himself with his arms to keep from freezing. A mumble
of words rises from his lips.*

bigger. Pshaw, nothing but that old piece of tin banging.
They ain't found me yet! From the first jump I out-figure
'em. (*Stopping.*) Uhm—everything sleepy and 'way off—
(*With sudden loudness.*) I ain't scared, naw. They all scared,
feeling me in the night, feel me walking behind 'em. . . .
And everywhere, the bulls is searching them old nigger
houses—Indiana, Calumet, Prairie, Wabash! Ha! But I ain't
'mong the niggers. (*Calling softly.*) Clara! (*He listens at the
door at the right.*) Why don't she come on here? (*He sinks
down on an old box and pulls his blanket shiveringly about
him. The flopping tin bangs off at the left. He springs instinctively and nervously up, then sits down again.*) Ain't

nothing—that old tin banging again, hanging loose and
ready to fall. Fall on down, old tin, but I ain't gonna fall.
They ain't gonna get me. (*Gazing back over his shoulder at
the night sky. Chuckling with low and bitter irony.*) They
smart, them white folks! Yeh, they get the niggers. But,
maybe not too smart— (*He spits in the air. He beats his arms
about him and stares out into the night.*) That's right! Flash
away, old sign! "Sun-kissed oranges." Ha! I'll be in them
orange-groves soon . . . with the sun on my back! (*He
raises his head more and sees far away, above him, the re-
volving beam of the beacon in the sky.*) Uhmm—an' look at
that old Lindbergh beacon, shining there 'way out through
the darkness— (*Musingly.*) Old Lindbergh—he knowed the
way. Boiling icy water below him, the thunder and the lightning, the freezing and the hail around him. Keep on driving
—riding through. (*Imitating the sound of an airplane pro-
peller with his numbed lips.*) V-r-r-r-rh-h-h-h! V-r-r-r-ruh-
uh-uh! Yes, he made it, got there. And all the people running
and shouting, and the headlights switching and sweeping the
sky! Old Lindbergh—he made it—got home, safe home. He
not scared! (*Snapping his head up, his hollow eyes burning
through the shadows before him.*) Aw, I ain't scared neither!
(*He laughs.*) An' when I light, ain't goin' to be no lot of people running to me with flowers! . . . no! When I come, they
run! Run like Hell! (*Laughs. And now from the depths of
the great city below comes the sound of a siren. He springs
around, the piece of rotted blanket falling from his shoulders.
He grips his gun tightly in his hand and crouching down,
moves swiftly to the window at the left. Inching his head up
against the sill, he peers over. The sound dies away. He turns
from the window.*) Sure, nothing but a' ambulance! Another
fool white man done broke his neck somewhere.

FOR ONE WOMAN

LADY IN WAITING [1]

by

MARGERY SHARP

MA *is a solicitous old soul. She is the mother of a renowned acrobatic troupe.*

MA. All according to taste, ain't it? Some likes country and some likes towns. . . . Give me London and I ask no more. . . . London's the best. I've toured the 'Ole Continong in me time, and never seen anything better than Victoria Station. I can smell it in me sleep. . . . And it ain't 'ard-'earted, like some cities. I tell you I'd rather be down and out in London than anywhere else on earth! . . . (I've never been down and out.) Not since I got married to Dad. Well, I was alive before then, wasn't I? (*Taking whole room in.*) Twenty-five years old, I was and kept myself for the last ten. That's the Genocchios all over! Fred, and 'is father, and my father-in-law, all just the same. They 'ate to think as how any of their wives 'ave ever been single. You know the sort. (*Slapping* ESME's *hand, familiarly.*) . . . Well, I'm on me way to visit friends. He won't come. He's going to spend the night all by 'imself, in an 'otel. . . . I'm going to some of the oldest friends I've got in the whole world, and Fred 'ere's too proud to eat 'is supper with 'em. . . . (*Addressing the gathering.*) I don't say they're in our class, they ain't, but they've a name, same as we 'ave. The Cocoloros—you may know it —no? They're retired now—but they've been in the business, father and son, for years and years—. . . . Well—they train fleas, dearie. Mind you, they don't make money in it like you used, but it's nothing to be ashamed of. And at any rate fleas ain't sexy—like some of these new turns.

HANDY MAN [1]

by

TOM POWERS

MRS. MITCHELL, though wealthy and widely traveled, has never lost her interest in small town affairs. She is happy to return to her native Louisville.

MRS. MITCHELL. Well, yes, in a way— You see, we used to live here until my husband went off to Mexico—that's where he died. . . . We don't know just where he's buried, so I never feel like a real widow because of that. My children were all born here, but they can hardly remember the town. . . . Nineteen years since we went to New York. Before we left here we lived on—we were poor then, you see—on lower Floyd Street. . . . That little house was my first home—my only home I think at times. I had a hard time when I was in it, and I've never been happy since I got out of it. Is it still there, just the same? . . . You say you've seen it—the little house? . . . He made those boxes himself. I never will forget while he was making them, the minister came to call—to caution him about some devilment he'd been up to. We was young then, of course—and he was always up to something. I was sittin' on the porch, patchin' the seat of my little boy's pants—he was sawin' and hammerin' and talkin'—he was sawin' and he got to tellin' the preacher a yarn about him and some other sailors that once took a Rocky Mountain jackass and painted it up like a zebra and presented it to an old Sultan as a gift from the gods so they could go free—and the preacher laughed so he forgot what he come for—and went off without scoldin' him. . . . Oh, I have to laugh now when I think of some of his pranks. . . . Nobody never understood him, I guess, but me and the dogs and the tramps. Even when I had to scold him, I couldn't help from laughin' at his pranks. Anybody living in the little house down there now?

FARM OF THREE ECHOES [1]

by

NOEL LANGLEY

The scene is OUMA's *home in Transvaal, South Africa. At 97 years of age,* OUMA's *mind tends to wander. The many years of hard and constant toil on the farm have formed a pattern, and she will be active until she dies.*

OUMA. Lisha, Isaac's plate was dirty. He'd have broken it if it had been him to see it and not me, and we'd be short when the Predikant comes on Wednesday. If it'd been him to see it and not me he'd have burned your finger over the candle again, and then I'd have to chop the wood until it mended. There's another thing: when I went up to the attic this afternoon Jan was playing in my coffin. . . . (*Doggedly as she crosses to center.*) When I went up to the attic Jan was playing in my coffin. . . . It's watered silk the lining, and him putting his bare feet all over it. . . . (*Sits by the fire.*) He's no right to go playing in the attic. It's my attic. And I forget where I hide the key. I never slept this afternoon for thinking of his feet where my head lay. . . . That watered silk cost eleven shillings the yard. Oupa rode all the way into Bloemfontein to fetch it. Oupa didn't have my coffin made of wal-

nut and lined with watered silk for Jan to wipe his feet on.
. . . He's nineteen. I married at fourteen. What's the matter with him? . . . Nine sons I gave Oupa and should have been eleven but for the two born dead the night of the rebellion. Nine sons, and of all of them only the youngest came back from Paul Kruger's war. Eight of my sons he took, Lisha. I was never told why he made them fight. But they took me to see him on his grey horse, and he shook my hand. Oom Paul shook my hand, Lisha. . . . They took me to see Paul Kruger in Pretoria once, Isaac and Oupa. He rode a grey horse and wore a top hat like the Predikant's. Before the war it was. Or after. . . . (*Suddenly.*) Lisha, where's my shawl? . . . I mean the grey lace one. . . . I had it on when I came in from the kitchen. Oupa bought it the same time as the china mug with Oom Paul's picture on it, and flags were on the other. . . . The flags got scraped off when it was washed. Have you found it, Lisha? . . .

THE BEAUTIFUL PEOPLE [1]

by

WILLIAM SAROYAN

AGNES—*Saint Agnes of the Mice, so-called because she knows that they are as much a part of the magnificence of the universe as men. In gratitude they spell her name in flowers.* AGNES *expects a lot of human beings, too. They must realize how long they've been here and what a responsibility it is. And then she meets the boy who held the door for her.*

AGNES. First we went out on the steps of the library, but we just stood there, too. We got in the way of some people who were in a hurry. About eleven of them. They didn't like us. Both of us. They turned around and looked at us. There were other people coming and going, too, and we were still in the way. When we got out of their way we were facing the same direction—we weren't facing each other. We were together. . . . I couldn't think of anything to say. I didn't think I'd be able to speak English even—and I suppose I didn't, after we did talk—what we said was so foolish. . . . We could barely walk. He kept bumping into me and I kept bumping into him, and he kept saying excuse me and I kept saying oh that's all right. He stumbled, too, and said something about his shoes. . . . He said they didn't fit. . . . I know he is a good boy, but now I don't understand anything. I began to see! I didn't used to see. The street cars going by had people in them suddenly. There have always been people in street cars, but now they were beautiful people. I never saw people that way before. They were still sad and funny and worried-looking, but now they were beautiful, too. We walked through the park and looked at everything together. It's not the same as looking at things alone. We looked at the pigeons, as if they had just come down from the sky. As if there had never been birds before. As if they came to be with us. . . . Oh, they're beautiful. They know people. They live in buildings. . . . They circled around and around. They pointed at them and said pigeons. I knew they were pigeons, but when he said they were—I liked him. And I knew what he meant, too. . . . I can't say what he meant, but I know what he meant. He didn't mean pigeons. He couldn't mean pigeons and say it so sadly. It was the same with everything else, too. Everybody in the street that we passed was new. They were like him. I felt sorry for them. I thought love would be another thing—not pity. Is pity love? . . . He's bewildered and shy and full of terrible sorrow, and his shoes don't fit. . . . (*Slowly, as if she were seeking the words.*) I've waited every day—to meet one person in the world— who wouldn't offend me—and now that I've found him— instead of being heedless—and strong—and full of humor— he's sad. He could be barefooted for all I care, if he wouldn't be sad—because now I'm sad, too. (*With youthful anger.*) I won't allow it. Pity's no seed to throw among the living. It's for mice, whose littleness rejoices with it. I can't believe to live—to really live—is foolish or impossible. (*In soft voice.*) Is it impossible, Father?

SWEET ALOES [1]

by

JAY MALLORY

LINDA *is an attractive 23. She lives with her maiden Aunt in a smug little English Village.*

LINDA. I never want to see the Bay again. . . . I don't want to think of it even. . . . You want me to tell you about—you know. . . . That morning? . . . Oliver called me into his room. He was standing by the window tying his tie. He said he'd never seen the Bay looking so beautiful. It really did seem to have some extra magic about it that day—shimmering essence of blue, and lazy smoke in the distance, and little dancing boats with coloured sails. . . . He had his arm around my shoulder, it was an exquisitely serene moment. Then I felt him slump away from me, and when I looked round he was lying on the floor. . . . Later, while I was waiting for the doctor and there was nothing to do, I looked out again—everything just the same, except that the boats had danced on a little further—but the whole scene was nothing but a shrieking reminder that Oliver wasn't there any more to share it.

[1] Copyright, 1937, by Jay Mallory.

THE CREAM IN THE WELL [1]

by

LYNN RIGGS

JULIE *returns to her father's farm to welcome her brother. She is tense, tormented by some inner violence which she can neither understand nor control.*

JULIE. (*Nervous and haunted.*) I've been thinking that—maybe I shouldn't have come. Maybe Clabe won't even speak to me. After what he said, I don't know. For a whole week now, I thought about it and thought about it. But I had to come, anyway! (*Absorbed.*) I hope I did right to come. Something happened to make me think so. Just as we started out, Smoky's colt came running up and before I could stop it, it ran out the gate. I couldn't get the wild little thing back. But I thought maybe he'd follow, all right. But he didn't follow, at all. *He led the way.* That colt was born here—but we took it away right after, you remember. And it's never been back. I kept wondering how it knew the way—every turn, every cross road, around the lake and to the left. It even dodged the barbed wire coiled up there in the dried grass where the old fence used to be. I had to drive fast to keep up with it. It was like something you read about, the way it snorted and pranced, and kept far ahead. I couldn't take my eyes off it all the way. (*With a wry laugh, becoming conscious of her curious excitement.*) I don't mean I felt like that colt exactly; but I suddenly found myself glad to be coming home. Knowing it was the right thing to do. Wondering why I'd put it off so long.

[1] Copyright, 1940, by Lynn Riggs.

GAS LIGHT [1] (ANGEL STREET)

by

PATRICK HAMILTON

Completely under the influence of her husband, MRS. MAN- NINGHAM *is being driven mad by him in the slow torturous manner which she describes.*

MRS. MANNINGHAM. Jack—I'm to make a last appeal to you. I'm going to make a last appeal. I'm desperate, Jack. Can't you see that I'm desperate? If you can't, you must have a heart of stone. . . . Jack, I may be going mad, like my poor mother—but if I am mad you have got to treat me gently. Jack . . . I never lie to you knowingly. If I have taken down that picture I have not known it. I have not known it. If I took it down on those other occasions I did not know it, either . . . Jack, if I steal your things—your rings—your keys—your pencils and your handkerchiefs, and you find them later at the bottom of my box, as indeed you do, then I do not know that I have done it. . . . Jack—if I commit these fantastic, meaningless mischiefs—so meaningless—why should I take a picture down from its place? If I do all these things, then I am certainly going off my head, and must be treated kindly and gently so that I may get well. You must bear with me, Jack, bear with me—not storm and rage. God knows I'm trying, Jack, I'm trying! . . . Believe that I'm trying, and be kind to me!

[1] Copyright, 1939, by Patrick Hamilton.

FOR TWO WOMEN

THE LADY HAS A HEART [1]

by

LADISLAUS BUS-FEKETE

CECILE, *a cheerful, good-natured person, wife of the Prime Minister of Budapest, has a visit with her beautiful, and at present, very agitated daughter.*

KATINKA *enters. Crosses to her mother in some agitation.*

CECILE. (*Greatly astonished.*) Katinka! What a surprise! When your father telephoned he didn't say he was bringing you with him.

KATINKA. I haven't come with Father.

CECILE. Why not?

KATINKA. I came alone—(*Takes off her coat.*) I absolutely had to speak to you, before Father got here from Parliament.

CECILE. (*Startled.*) Has anything happened?

KATINKA. Mother, I was in the House of Parliament this morning.

CECILE. Since when have you been going to Parliament?

KATINKA. (*Exploding.*) Since our manservant has become a regular attendant there. There must be at least one member of the family who takes the doings of that man seriously.

CECILE. Your father is so wise. If he has no objections to his activity, I feel reassured.

KATINKA. (*Harassed. Sits center. On bench.*) That's the hitch —for years it has been the opinion of the family that Father is wise, while in reality dear Father makes one silly mistake after another—and- that fellow Jean is cunning enough to take every unfair advantage because he knows Father so well.

CECILE. My child! If anyone were to hear you—

KATINKA. Mother, I don't want to hurt you. But things can't go on like this. You've been here on the estate for the last three months.

CECILE. (*A little apologetically.*) It's so comfortable here—

KATINKA. You don't even read a newspaper, so you don't know that we're the laughing-stock of the whole country.

CECILE. Then I've been very sensible not to read the newspapers and fret myself.

KATINKA. In the Budgetary debate today, that fellow Jean delivered such a speech that at last there wasn't a single Minister left in the hall. They'd all run away.

CECILE. My dear, what could gentlemen do—

KATINKA. Only Father remained there, calmly sitting there in his seat and smiling. Why, he very nearly applauded Jean.

CECILE. Then it must have been a very good speech.

KATINKA. (*Rises and crosses to left platform.*) Father! Wise Father—you'll see—the end of it all will be that Father will be driven out of office by his own manservant.

CECILE. Tell me, child. Since when have you taken so much interest in politics?

KATINKA. I'm not in the least interested in politics. I've never been one of the women who want to vote. Oh, but if only I had been able to vote in the last elections—I would have shown him.

CECILE. With one little feminine vote?

KATINKA. Mother, I can't simply ignore the machinations of this servant fellow any longer.

CECILE. That's all we can do, dear, ignore him.

KATINKA. But don't you understand? At home he ties Father's cravat, and in Parliament he tries to cut his throat. At home he opens every door for Father, and in Parliament he does all he can to slam doors in his face. And the health and strength and energy for all this he derives from your admittedly excellent kitchen.

CECILE. Well, the food in the servants' hall is really not so particularly good. Of course I could cut down on it a bit. But I'd hate to resort to such a mean little trick.

KATINKA. (*Crosses to her Mother.*) Please take note of the fact that I've come down here expressly for the purpose of having that creature turned out of the house immediately.

CECILE. Katinka! I've never seen you in such a state of mind before. Tant de bruit! Why is it you hate this man so?

KATINKA. Hate him? (*Sits on bench.*) Yes, I hate him! In the morning when I wake up, my first thought is that I hate him, and in the evening I can't sleep for hating him! Just fancy, the other evening I saw him at the opera. He seemed to be having his night off. He was sitting in the second row— A better seat than mine.

CECILE. He's sure to have gotten a free ticket. Members of Parliament can get them very easily.

KATINKA. (*Passionately.*) He was wearing a dark blue lounge suit.

CECILE. For economy, dear. I'm sure for economy. Even the cheap ones look well.

KATINKA. No! Such a faultless dark blue lounge suit that I thought I must kill him on the spot. I have such instincts at times. This morning, in Parliament, when I was sitting in the gallery, I suddenly had the feeling—now—now—I must throw my bag at his head. Believe me, it's only since this man has been occupying my thoughts that I've discovered how temperamental I can be.

CECILE. Yes, my child. Sometimes one has certain feelings in regard to certain men.

KATINKA. I've never had such feelings about any man—I've only had them about—well—I've just never had them before— Oh, if only I were a man!—and could coolly, calmly—quietly—scratch his eyes out—

CECILE. Now that you've brought up the subject—I'm not ashamed to tell you about myself—I, too, have been occupying myself with this man Jean— Yes, I have—

KATINKA. But Mother, I expressed myself badly—I haven't been occupying myself with him. He revolts me—

CECILE. Oh, he doesn't revolt me. To the contrary—

KATINKA. Then you're very disloyal to me, and to Father.

CECILE. I've never read serious books. I've never had the ambition to be a famous, clever woman. Problems haven't fascinated me. The world at large hasn't interested me. I've always contented myself with our own small intimate circle.

KATINKA. Which has been betrayed!

CECILE. Here no stranger could ever intrude—

KATINKA. He isn't a stranger!

CECILE. And so I've passed my life in the conviction that only we are the people, so to speak—and that the others, well—whether they were servants—lawyers—artisans, well, the others don't count, that's all.

KATINKA. There are some who think they do.

CECILE. And then this fellow, Jean. I know quite well that he is the son of a manservant and a peasant girl, but to my tremendous surprise he suddenly began to speak, and it turns out that he reads, he studies, he educates himself. He pronounces foreign words faultlessly.

KATINKA. Naturally! He's had us to listen to!

CECILE. Well, he can debate as well as your husband can. Indeed, sometimes he says far cleverer things—

KATINKA. We shall see to it that he doesn't do it any more.

CECILE. I couldn't help thinking that these journalists who are constantly writing such a heap about people being equal —that perhaps they are right after all. Believe me, my child, it has confused me a bit.

KATINKA. I'm not confused! My course of action is perfectly plain. I shall wait only to speak to Father, and inquire if he wishes to perform the obvious family duty.

OLD ACQUAINTANCE [1]

by

John van Druten

KIT MARKHAM, *a brilliant writer, and* MILDRED DRAKE *a popular novelist, have been friends over such a long period of years that they are able to withstand any situation.*

MILLY. (*As she comes in.*) What's the matter with Sabrina? Keeping me waiting like that.

KIT. I suppose she was busy in the kitchen.

MILLY. (*Shaking out her furs.*) It's just started snowing. I think we're going to have a blizzard. Have you heard from Deirdre today?

KIT. What? . . . Yes, I heard from her.

MILLY. Where was she? What did she say?

KIT. She'd been to the movies. She said that you'd . . . evicted her.

MILLY. (*Somewhat taken aback.*) I haven't evicted her at all. I've just bowed out. You've won, Kit. I give up. That's what I came here to tell you. I just wanted you to know. I'm not staying.

KIT. Oh, aren't you?

MILLY. It's no good arguing with me. My mind's made up. I'm going back to Pelham. Miss Harrison and cook and Annie and Susan are up there now, getting the place ready.

KIT. Milly, you haven't bowed out; you've swept out! And what's Deirdre supposed to be going to do?

MILLY. Just what she's always wanted to do. Stay here in New York . . . with you. Go places with you. Live the life she's always wanted . . . with you.

KIT. Yes, but I'm afraid that's not going to be possible now.

MILLY. Because of your getting married?

KIT. No, not because of that.

MILLY. Why not, then? (SABRINA *comes in with tea things*.) Why isn't it going to be possible?

KIT. (*Indicating* SABRINA *with her head*.) I'll tell you later.

MILLY. Tell me now.

KIT. (*As before.*) Later.

MILLY. (*Getting the idea at last.*) Oh, all right. I wasn't expecting tea.

KIT. It was Sabrina's idea.

MILLY. Thank you, Sabrina. (*To* KIT, *making conversation, while* SABRINA *serves the tea*.) I . . . er . . . brought your book back.

KIT. Oh, yes.

MILLY. You say you're still revising it?

KIT. Yes.

MILLY. Well, I think it needs it . . . here and there. There are two whole chapters that I think could come right out.

KIT. (*Instinctively defensive*.) Which?

MILLY. The ones where you analyze her diaries. They hold up your story. We've had the diaries. We don't want to know what you think of them.

KIT. Oh, but . . .

MILLY. Either you write novels, or you write psychoanalysis. You don't do both.

KIT. Oh, but . . . (*Then slowly*.) No, you're perfectly right. Of course they can go out. They should go out. Thank you, Milly.

SPRING MEETING [1]

by

M. H. FARRELL AND JOHN PERRY

JOAN *and* BABY *are despairing over the clothes situation. They live in Ireland in an old house that was once the scene of more prosperous days.*

[1] Copyright, 1938, by M. J. Farrell and John Perry.

JOAN. It has that look as if it came to Dublin from Liberty. They got tired of dusting it month after month with a feather brush.

BABY. So they said, "Oh, what the . . . we'll send it to Ireland with the out-sizes."

JOAN. It's a swine.

BABY. So big, isn't it?

JOAN. Not considering Cousin Maud weighs fourteen stone and eats all round her. (*She digs in a row of pins.*)

BABY. (*In front of the mirror.*) Oh, darling, me that time. Joan, darling, if we took a couple of darts in it here, would that be a better line?

JOAN. (*Crossing to the chair up left for scissors.*) You get five shillings out of father and take it along to that wonderful little woman, Madam Murphy. (*She comes down to behind* BABY.) Perhaps she's not Schiaparelli, but then am I?

BABY. What a hope I have of getting five shillings out of Sir Richard. Besides, you know I owe Miss Murphy twenty-seven and six for the last year. I daren't go near her. (*She crosses to the mantelpiece for sweets.*)

JOAN. You said you'd settled that. (*She sits on the stool again.*)

BABY. Well, I couldn't. I owed Miss Brennan nearly three pounds for sweets and cigarettes, you see.

JOAN. Have you paid her?

BABY. I have paid her a bit on account, yes. . . . (*She crosses back to the mirror.*) Joan, this dress is awful. It's frightful, it's terrible. I wonder if James would lend me five shillings. (*She moves towards the passage up left.*)

JOAN. Wait now. (*She rises and cuts off bags of darts with scissors.*) With a nice little spray on the shoulder you won't know it.

BABY. Won't I? You'd be surprised. (*She moves to the chair down left.*)

JOAN. Oh, Baby, I am trying. Really! And it's not as bad as you think.

BABY. You're too darling, and patient with me. But, oh, Joanie, Joanie, it's such a cruel colour.

JOAN. (*Sitting on the stool.*) It's quite different by nightlight, silly. Turn round. And your skin can stand a lot. When I was your age I had spots as well as everything else to do battle against.

BABY. (*At mirror.*) That is better now. . . . You are a comfort. What would I do without you? How you could contend with father and Bijou all by yourself! But I suppose Aunt Bijou wasn't quite so crackers then?

JOAN. (*Who is again attending to the frock.*) Stand still, darling, or I'll stick you again.

BABY. Oh, that is improving. What do you think about the length? Leave it?

JOAN. (*Rising and moving around her.*) I'll just see what a lift on the shoulders will do. That hemline looks rather beyond me.

BABY. Oh, if we could only buy ourselves some nice new clothes. I wouldn't mind how cheap as long as they were new.

JOAN. And didn't smell of Cousin Maud.

BABY. It's quite an expensive smell, but it makes me sick.

JOAN. Me too. It's because we've had so many bitter contests with dresses that smell like this.

BABY. Just such a little money. Half what father spends on one of those dreary race-horses that never win a race, and I wouldn't call the King my aunt. All the same, Joan, I don't think I'll ever feel so bitter about it all as you do. I can't help liking him.

JOAN. Wait till you're thirty-two and then talk.

BABY. I don't know how we've stuck it out here so long. I must sit down a minute. (*She sits on the stool.*) Year after year always the same fight for a hot bath or the car to go to a tennis party.

JOAN. (*Sitting on the chair down left.*) Doling out tea and sugar to the kitchen. All the fruit sold out of the garden.

BABY. Not a strawberry for the house.

JOAN. Never a drink or a party. Nothing but doing the flowers and fighting with Bijou and growing older. . . . I'll never forget it, Baby. My first grand dance, and Bijou and father let me go in a sort of a tennis dress.

BABY. Blue?

JOAN. Blue.

BABY.
JOAN. } (*Together.*) A girl is always safe in blue.

(BABY *lights* JOAN's *cigarette and sits beside her on the settee.*)

JOAN. Clothes were expensive just after the war, and chaps were scarce. I think I danced three times—or did I? Anyhow, I wanted to die. I never wanted to die so much. . . . Well, I cried in the cloakroom. That was my date.

BABY. All the same, darling, I wish we had two boys to go with to-morrow night. We've shared poor Michael so often. Of course, I adore going to dances with Michael. He's adorable. He's grand. He's tall. He's dark. He's—oh, ooooo, but he's not mine. He's yours, Joanie.

JUPITER LAUGHS [1]

by

A. J. CRONIN

MARY, *a young medical school graduate, has come to Hopewell Towers to earn enough money for her fare to China where she wants to be a medical missionary.* JENNIE *is a sweet country girl.*

MARY *in white jacket, stethoscope in pocket, is gaily arranging in vases a large bunch of wild daffodils. Enter* JENNIE. *She carries a large sheet of white blotting paper, which she places on the table.*

MARY. What's that for?

JENNIE. For the meeting this afternoon, Miss. It's in here at three o'clock. (JENNIE *is just crossing upstage when* MARY *notices that her hand is wrapped in a handkerchief.*)

MARY. What have you done to your hand, Jennie?

JENNIE. Cut it on a tin, Miss.

MARY. Here, let's have a look at it.

JENNIE. 'Tisn't nothing, Miss. I ran the cold tap on it.

MARY. (*Examining the finger.*) It's deep; and you may get it dirty. You'd better get Matron to put some iodine on it.

JENNIE. (*Pulling hand away.*) Oh no, Miss.

MARY. Surely you're not frightened of iodine, are you?

JENNIE. Well, it isn't so much the iodine—as who puts it on, Miss.

MARY. All right; then run upstairs to my ward and ask Sister to do it for you. As a matter of fact, I believe Dr. Venner's around there somewhere. You can ask him if you like.

JENNIE. Oh, I wouldn't ask him, Miss. I wouldn't dare.

MARY. Why not? He won't eat you.

JENNIE. I know that, Miss. He's nice to me, he is. Always says good-morning and that. But he's so clever and everything. (*Then.*) Some of the others don't like him so much. But I do.

MARY. Good for you, Jennie.

JENNIE. I was glad when you and him got engaged, Miss. It didn't seem like we'd ever have anything of that here. Just like a film, isn't it?

MARY. I'm glad you're pleased, Jennie.

JENNIE. Everyone is. Even Matron. And you don't find almost nothing to please her.

MARY. (*Surprised.*) Matron was pleased!

JENNIE. Yes, Miss; "That's fine," she said; and then turned round and bit my head off for staring at her. Nasty old thing.

MARY. (*Laughing, in spite of herself.*) S-sh! Jennie!

JENNIE. Well, it's true, Miss.

MARY. I daresay; but it doesn't do to say so. Besides, you have to make allowances for people.

JENNIE. I'm afraid of her.

MARY. So am I, a little, Jennie.

JENNIE. Are you, Miss?—I suppose everyone is—except Dr. Venner.

MARY. (*Thoughtfully.*) Yes. (*A pause.*) Jennie.

JENNIE. Yes, Miss?

MARY. (*After a moment's hesitation.*) Matron doesn't like Dr. Venner, does she? I mean—she didn't even before I came here?

JENNIE. No, Miss. She's always been the same with him. She hates him worst of all. But he's got an answer for her every time.

MARY. Yes, that's the trouble— (*A pause.*) Jennie.

JENNIE. Yes, Miss?

MARY. Would you do something for me?

JENNIE. Yes, Miss.

MARY. I know it's wrong to repeat things or tell tales; but I'm sure this is different. If you ever heard anyone say anything about Dr. Venner that made you think they were trying to do him any harm, you would tell me, wouldn't you?

JENNIE. Of course, Miss. D'you mean trying to kill him, Miss?

MARY. (*Laughing in spite of her anxiety.*) Good heavens, no! Nothing like that! You're very bloodthirsty. There are lots of other ways they could hurt him.

JENNIE. Yes, Miss. Of course I'd tell you.

MARY. And you won't mention it?

JENNIE. Oh, no, Miss. It'll be a secret like between us We'll both look after him.

MARY. Thank you, Jennie. And now you'd better run along before you do anything else and ask Sister from me to do your hand for you.

JENNIE. Yes, Miss. Thank you, Miss. (*Exits* JENNIE *up left.*)

JUNE MAD [1]

by

FLORENCE RYERSON AND COLIN CLEMENTS

PENNY *is fifteen and in love. She has managed to beg, borrow or steal enough money to buy a party dress that is so "bad" it defies description.* MRS. WOOD *is an attractive woman, who fortunately has a sense of humor.*

PENNY. Forever, dear love—for ever and ever . . . (*Evidently she is not quite content with her rendition, for she gives a double hitch to the bodice of her dress, then tries it again, arms extended.*) Forever, dear love—for ever and ever . . . (*During the last part of this speech,* MRS. WOOD *enters from the dining room. She stands transfixed.*)

MRS. WOODS. Penelope! (PENNY *is taken completely off her guard. Instinctively, her hands go flying up to cover her bare shoulders.*)

PENNY. (*Turning slowly.*) I—yes, Mother.

MRS. WOOD. When did you get that dress?

PENNY. (*Forcing her arms down.*) This—this afternoon.

MRS. WOOD. Did your father—

PENNY. (*Quickly.*) No, he didn't! So you needn't scold him! And you needn't worry about the money, either. I got it by a perfectly honest business transaction!

MRS. WOOD. We won't talk about that now. I want you to go up-stairs this minute and take it off.

PENNY. No! No! I can't! I haven't anything else to wear.

MRS. WOOD. You have your last summer's party dress.

PENNY. But I can't wear that awful rag! Why, it's too tight.

And it's got sleeves! And it makes me look ten years old! . . .

MRS. WOOD. Penny, please don't get so excited.

PENNY. I'm not excited. I'm just desperate! How'd you feel if you saw another woman trying to get Father away from you?

MRS. WOOD. Penny! Hush! Someone might hear you! . . . Wait, Penny.

PENNY. I've got to go! You don't know what Julie's doing to him!

MRS. WOOD. (*Gently but firmly pushing* PENNY *down on the couch.*) She couldn't do it if he didn't let her.

PENNY. (*Becoming more and more upset.*) She could! Because she's older—and she knows how. Look at the way she winds Mervyn right around her finger! And makes her father run errands! (*Rises and moves left.*) And I've got to learn to act the way she does! I've got to be a woman of the world!

MRS. WOOD. Is that your ambition, Penny? I thought you wanted to be a writer.

PENNY. (*Turning around.*) Well, how'm I going to be a writer if I don't have anything to write? How'm I ever going to learn about life if you won't let me live?

MRS. WOOD. But, Penny, you are living . . . every day . . . every hour.

PENNY. That's not living—school, and tennis, and fencing with Chuck. That's just existing. Living's being in love, and feeling, and wanting things, and fighting for them. . . . (*With a strange, repressed hysteria.*) Listen! You're my mother. You can make me go back upstairs. You can make me put on that old last-year's party dress with sleeves. But I'm warning you, if you do, I'll never forgive you—never, as long as I live!

MRS. WOOD. (*As though thinking deeply.*) No—I don't believe you ever would.

PENNY. (*Moving closer.*) Can't you see I'm not a baby any more? I'm growing up! (*As* MRS. WOOD *remains silent and troubled*.) Mother, don't stand there like that! Are you going to be mean and cruel and send me back upstairs, or are you going to let me go out?

MRS. WOOD. (*Slowly, sadly.*) I'm going to be mean and cruel —and let you go out.

PENNY. (*Incredulous with joy.*) Mother—darling!

MORNING'S AT SEVEN [1]

by

PAUL OSBORN

CORA SWANSON, *living in a small town, has always had her sister,* ARRY, *in her home.* ESTHER, *another sister, is married to the eccentric* DAVID.

CORA. (*Turns to* ESTY—*they smile at each other—both sit on porch steps.*) It's good to see you, Esty. You don't have to get right back, do you?

ESTHER. David'll be back from his walk in a little while. I want to be there before he is. Carl hasn't come back yet, has he?

CORA. Not yet.

ESTHER. Ida phoned me. She wants me to talk to him if he's acting bad.

CORA. Oh, I think he'll be all right. It's just one of those dentist spells.

ESTHER. Well, I've seen those dentist spells when they got pretty bad sometimes. It's only one step from a dentist spell to a "Where am I" spell, you know.

CORA. Now, Esty! Carl's not going to have a "Where am I" spell!

ESTHER. I certainly hope not.

[1] Copyright, 1939, by Paul Osborn under the title "Summer Solstice." Copyright, 1940, by Paul Osborn.

CORA. Why, he hasn't had one of those in years and years.

ESTHER. Well, we can't do anything until he gets back. I'll talk to him. Maybe if he isn't too far gone it might help some. —Now tell me. Have you met Myrtle yet?

CORA. I haven't really met her. I just talked to her a second.

ESTHER. (*Controlling a giggle.*) What's she like?

CORA. (*Giggling nervously.*) Now, Esty! She's very nice! Not the way we imagined at all!

ESTHER. She has got teeth like this though, hasn't she?

CORA. Now, Esty, she has no such thing!

ESTHER. And she talks like this to Homer. (*They both giggle.*)

CORA. She doesn't either! She's perfectly all right! And we shouldn't sit here and giggle about it!

ESTHER. I can't help it! Somehow the idea of Homer's having a girl—

CORA. You know what Arry thinks? Well, Arry thinks that maybe everything isn't as straight there as it might be.

ESTHER. Well, maybe it isn't. Wonderful things can happen.

CORA. Esty! (*This sends them into a mild case of hysterics.*)

ESTHER. (*She wipes her eyes.*) My goodness, I haven't laughed so much for a long time.

CORA. That's right. How is David behaving?

ESTHER. Oh, I don't know, Cora. This last week I've hardly been out of the house.

CORA. I think it's a shame.

ESTHER. He made me promise I'd never come down again without his permission.

CORA. You didn't promise him—?

ESTHER. Well—I—I really had to. He said— (*She gives a nervous giggle.*) He said if I ever came down again I'd—I'd have to live on the second floor the rest of my life.

CORA. Live on the second floor?

ESTHER. Upstairs. And he'd live downstairs.

CORA. But that's silly, Esty! You couldn't live on the second floor.

ESTHER. I guess I'd have to. The house divided, you know.

CORA. How would you get your meals?

ESTHER. He says I can come down the backstairs and use the kitchen when I want it.

CORA. If that isn't just like David! Why doesn't he live on the second floor?

ESTHER. He thought it would be easier for me on account of the bathroom.

CORA. Oh! Well, what would he do for a bathroom?

ESTHER. He'd have another put in. In that little closet off the kitchen.

CORA. But that would cost money, Esty!

ESTHER. I know it would. That's the one thing that worries me. He says maybe I'd let him use the bath now and then.

CORA. (*Sharply.*) Well, I wouldn't!

ESTHER. Oh, I'd have to.—He says he'll put up a bell that will. ring when he wants to use it. So we wouldn't bump into each other.

CORA. And you wouldn't see each other at all?

ESTHER. I guess not. He says if we're going to be independent we might as well be independent. Of course if we should meet in the hall we'd bow to each other, like two acquaintances.

CORA. Well, he's just trying to scare you, Esty. And I think you ought to take a stand against him! You ought to be able to come down here any time you want to. David's just jealous!

ESTHER. I know it, Cora. He gets more so all the time. If he'd only stop talking about his Crystal Fortress.

CORA. You know, Esty, I always thought that Crystal Fortress was rather a lovely idea.

ESTHER. You wouldn't if you'd lived in it fifty-five years.

CORA. No, I think it's lovely. Your friends or anybody can come up to the fortress and look in through the door—and you can see them and talk with them and everything—but no one can ever really come into it except just the two of you. Just you two all alone there by yourselves. It must be nice sometimes to be all alone with—the person you live with. (*Pause.* ESTHER *sits watching* CORA. *Suddenly* CORA *turns on her and says with surprising viciousness.*) Esty! I hope Homer doesn't marry Myrtle!

ESTHER. What!

CORA. Oh, I know it's selfish of me! But I hope he doesn't!

ESTHER. But why, Cora?

CORA. Because if he doesn't, Carl has promised to let me have that house up on Sycamore Drive, to lease it to me for as long as I want.

ESTHER. But what would you want with that house?

CORA. I want to live in it! I want for Thor and me to live in it! All by ourselves.

ESTHER. And this house?

CORA. Arry can have it! She can have everything that's in it!

ESTHER. I see.

CORA. Wouldn't it be wonderful, Esty?

ESTHER. Yes, I suppose it would, Cora.

CORA. (*Pause.* CORA *feels* ESTHER *staring at her.*) Of course, I suppose it would make Arry good and mad.

ESTHER. Do you think Thor will do it?

CORA. Well, I—I don't know. I haven't asked him yet, of course.

ESTHER. When is Carl going to let you know?

CORA. Well, Carl says that if Homer doesn't say definitely that he's going to get married while Myrtle's here—that is, set an actual date and all—well, Carl thinks Homer never will marry her and then I can have the house. I've got the lease all drawn up, right here. All he's got to do is sign it.

MRS. MOONLIGHT [1]

by

Benn W. Levy

MINNIE *of the unconciliatory countenance perched upon so nondescript a little body is completely devoted to her dear, pretty* MRS. MOONLIGHT. *It is the year 1881.*

SARAH. Minnie. (*She is speaking half to herself.*) I don't know what will become of me.

MINNIE. Of course you don't. Which of us does?

SARAH. I'm never— (*She has difficulty in saying it aloud.*) I'm never going to look any older.

MINNIE. What rubbish is this! (MINNIE *is not at ease.*)

SARAH. (*Almost a cry.*) It's true. I know it. I know it. I suppose I've really known it for some time.

MINNIE. Ah, away with you!

SARAH. But I didn't think it would matter.

MINNIE. And nor it would.

SARAH. Then you know, too, it's true?

MINNIE. Indeed, I know no such nonsense!

SARAH. (*Meaningly.*) Your necklace, Minnie.

MINNIE. What about my stupid old necklace? (*This is a nasty moment for* MINNIE.)

SARAH. And the legend?

MINNIE. I tell you I know no legend.

SARAH. One wish to every owner?

MINNIE. Why do you plague your head with that fallydiddle?

SARAH. I wished, Minnie. It was just before Jane was born, and I used to wear your necklace always. (MINNIE *is dabbing at her eyes with a corner of her apron.*) I was afraid that, when Jane was born, I might not be so pretty, and Tom might love me less. So I wished and wished that I might never look any older. (*There is silence for a moment.*) I wished and I

wished. That legend, Minnie; it's not fallydiddle, is it?
MINNIE. Don't plague me! How should I know?
SARAH. But you don't think so, do you? (*Miserably, poor*
MINNIE *shakes her head.*) I suppose it was wicked of me to
wish. Vain and unnatural. Now I—I'm a kind of—freak.
MINNIE. (*Breaking out.*) Don't torment yourself, my dar-
ling! It's not true, and, if it is, think how lucky you are! To
be your own pretty self always!
SARAH. (*Still following her own train of thought.*) A witch.
We have new methods of burning witches. We burn their
dear ones too. Minnie.
MINNIE. What is it, angel, what is it?
SARAH. If ever you should get a letter from me—ever, do you
hear?
MINNIE. Yes, yes, dear, I hear.
SARAH. Everything in it you must treat as sacred. Not a soul
must see it but you. No one else must know what's in it.
MINNIE. And what will be in it?
SARAH. The—the truth. Will you promise?
MINNIE. But why should you start writing me letters? When
would you have cause?
SARAH. Probably never—but promise!
MINNIE. Of course I promise; but let's forget all about it.

EIGHT O'CLOCK TUESDAY [1]

by

ROBERT WALLSTEN AND MIGNON G. EBERHART

*Re-enacting to the last detail events preceding the murder
of* IVAN GODDEN, *his wife,* MARCIA, *and his sister reveal a conversation they had prior to the crime.*

BEATRICE. (*Coming to front of desk*.) Wasn't that Rob Copley who just left?

MARCIA. Yes, Beatrice.

BEATRICE. I suppose you think I haven't noticed you and Rob since Ivan's been in the hospital.

MARCIA. Have you?

BEATRICE. Do you think it quite decent to carry on with him right in your husband's house?

MARCIA. How can you say that?

BEATRICE. It's got to stop, Marcia. I don't know how far it's gone, but it's got to stop.

MARCIA. Beatrice—will you let me tell you something? I love him—terribly.

BEATRICE. (*Sits.*) And so you want to leave Ivan—

MARCIA. Yes. (*Sits on footstool.*)

BEATRICE. Well, you're not the only woman in the world who has wanted to do that! And do you really think you can?

MARCIA. I only know I can't put an end to it. Probably you don't understand, Beatrice, but I can't.

BEATRICE. Understand? If you really love him, nothing can put an end to it. No matter how hard you try, it goes on and on, just as deep and just as sharp as long as you live. But you must stop seeing him.

MARCIA. No. I'm going to ask Ivan for a divorce— This evening when he comes home.

BEATRICE. He's coming home this evening?

MARCIA. I haven't had a chance to tell you— He's probably on the way.

BEATRICE. So it will all start again. (*Pause.*) The fire's going down, Marcia. Fix it. (MARCIA *rises and goes up to fireplace*, BEATRICE *follows her; goes above desk*.) Marcia, don't ask Ivan for a divorce. You don't know him even yet. He'll stoop to anything—anything to keep you from Rob. He did that to me once, a long time ago, with a horrible lie. When I knew what he had done, I went upstairs and locked myself in my room— And then years later, when the man came back and asked me to forgive him, it was too late.

MARCIA. Oh, Beatrice—
BEATRICE. I told you this only to warn you. You mustn't try to fight Ivan. He's always the stronger. If they're on the way, I'd better see that his room is ready.

FOR TWO MEN

ONE MAD NIGHT [1]

by

JAMES REACH

DON CUTTER, *a young playwright, comes to the Cutter Mansion to finish his latest play, and finds* DR. BUNN *and his patients.*

DR. BUNN. Now, gentlemen—what can I do for you?

DON. I wonder. I suppose I'd better introduce myself. I'm Mother Goo— I'm Don Cutter. And this is Wing.

DR. BUNN. How do you do?

DON. Is this the Cutter house, or am I crazy too?

DR. BUNN. (*Laughing.*) It is and you aren't.

DON. Then I own it. I'm a playwright, or at least I think I am, and I came here for peace and quiet—to write in an atmosphere of calm and seclusion.

DR. BUNN. I see. It's most unfortunate that you came at this time.

DON. This time?

DR. BUNN. Let me explain—

DON. I wish you would.

DR. BUNN. Well, you see, I own a home for mental cases on the other side of the hill. Or, rather, I did own it—

DON. You don't own it now?

DR. BUNN. What's left of it. It was practically destroyed by fire last night.

DON. I understand. So you—er—borrowed this?

DR. BUNN. Well, yes. I knew it hadn't been used for years. It never occurred to me that anyone was likely to show up. Of course, I'd be willing to pay any reasonable rental while my own place is being repaired. This is just what I need. In mental cases, you know, seclusion is quite vital—

DON. And quiet.

DR. BUNN. Precisely.

DON. Yes. Well, under the circumstances, I suppose the only thing for us to do is clear out—

DR. BUNN. Oh, I hardly think that would be necessary. It seems a shame for you, after coming all the way up here. Why don't you stay on, for a while at least?

DON. Thank you. I don't quite fancy being boiled in oil.

DR. BUNN. They're really quite harmless. I can assure you you won't be molested again. There's plenty of room—you could have a whole wing to yourself. The house is big and there's only seven of us.

DON. Seven?

DR. BUNN. Yes. Myself, Mrs. Kluck, the housekeeper; Lady Macbeth; John and Priscilla; and— (*The woman's scream is heard again.*)

DON. And Lucille!

DR. BUNN. Eh?

DON. Lucille. Priscilla told me about her.

DR. BUNN. Yes? What did she tell you?

DON. Oh—er—nothing—just her name.

DR. BUNN. A sad case—very sad.

DON. Sadder than the others?

DR. BUNN. So young—and beautiful.

DON. I see.

DR. BUNN. Poor girl—poor girl!

DON. I think I will stay, Doc—

DR. BUNN. Fine.

DON. Until the morning, in any case. Then we can see.

DR. BUNN. As you wish. Your man will find some food in the kitchen—

DON. He has found it.

DR. BUNN. Good. You'll find the west wing empty—to your

right at the head of the stairs. And now, if you'll pardon me,
I'll say goodnight.

DON. Goodnight, Doc.

ABIE'S IRISH ROSE [1]

by

ANNE NICHOLS

ABIE *is a young, likeable Jewish boy who has fallen in love
and married an Irish girl. He has brought her home to meet
his father.* SOLOMON *is delighted with* ROSE MARY, *believing
her to be of his faith.*

ABIE. You like her, Dad?

SOLOMON. She's a nice girl, Jewish and everything.

ABIE. (*Not so sure.*) Yeh!

SOLOMON. How much money has she got?

ABIE. Oh, I don't know exactly. Her father is comfortably
fixed, that is all I know.

SOLOMON. And your father is comfortably fixed, too! (*Smiling knowingly.*)

ABIE. What do you mean?

SOLOMON. You like her, don'd you?

ABIE. Do I! (*This speaks volumes.*)

SOLOMON. Who could help it?

ABIE. Do you really like her, Dad?

SOLOMON. She's a nice girl. Didn't I told you to vait ven you
brought all those girls around, those Christian girls? Didn't
I say "Abie, vait—someday you'll meet a nize little Jewish
girl." Didn't I say that?

ABIE. You did, Dad!

SOLOMON. Uh—Bahama, aren't you glad you vaited?

ABIE. I'm glad I waited for Rose Mary!

SOLOMON. (*Grabs his hand angrily, almost yelling at him.*) Please don'd call her Rose Mary. (*Smiles.*) She's Rosie!

ABIE. All right—Rosie! But I don't care what she is; it's the girl I like, not her religion.

SOLOMON. Sure—fine! You don'd care, but I care! We'll have no "Schickies" in this family. (*He hits table.*)

ABIE. You mean to say if Rosie were a Christian you wouldn't like her?

SOLOMON. Bud she isn't!

ABIE. Oh, piffle!

SOLOMON. (*Getting angry.*) Don'd you peefle me!

ABIE. I didn't mean it for you—

SOLOMON. (*Hitting table. Paying no attention to* ABIE's *semi-apology.*) I von'd be peefled!

ABIE. (*Meekly.*) All right.

SOLOMON. No sir! (ABIE *says nothing, sits with his hands deep in his pockets, hunched down in chair.*)

SOLOMON. Positivil! Ein umglik mit dem ziem meinen zoog ich azoi zoogt er azoi shut up. (ABIE *still says nothing.* SOLOMON *talks long strings of Jewish, then awakes to the fact that he is arguing against the wind; he looks at* ABIE. ABIE *pays no attention—seems lost in his own thoughts.*) Vhy don'd you say something?

ABIE. There is nothing to say.

SOLOMON. Don'd argue with me. You get a nice little Jewish girl and you don'd hang on to her.

ABIE. (*With double meaning.*) I'm hanging on to her all right!

SOLOMON. Yeh, all right vhy don'd you marry her qvick?

ABIE. Dad, have I your consent?

SOLOMON. Do you vant me to ask her for you?

ABIE. No. I can do that.

SOLOMON. Vell do it, and—if she says yes, I'll start you in some kind of a business. What would you like?

ABIE. I hate business.

SOLOMON. You'll need a business ven you start raising a fambly! Esk Rosie! She's got a common senses!

ABIE. (*Apprehensively.*) Say, Dad—don't mention anything about a family to Rose Mary.

SOLOMON. (*Grabs head angrily.*) Oi—ich platz. Didn't I just tell you not to call her dod Rose Mary. (*Smiles.*) She's Rosie!

ABIE. All right, Rosie!

THE WEAK LINK [1]

by

ALLAN WOOD

PETER *is a simple sincere young man. He has a theory that every bank has a weak link. He believes he is talking with The Bankers Protective Agency. In reality it is a "front" for a group of bank robbers headed by* KING. DOC *is a mean little man, untrustworthy.*

PETER. (*At phone.*) Hello! Gale? Where are you? Gale! I've got a job— I say I've got a— Did you tell anybody I was up here in—you know where? You didn't? Well, don't. This is a very secretive business, Gale. I'm going to have charge of the Third District. We're going to discuss salary now. What? Of course you can come up. That's what I wanted to tell— What? No, dear, I don't want you to say anything about my salary. We'll take anything they offer— No, I don't think that is silly— Come right up. And Gale—see that you are not followed. Goodbye. We're keeping our money downstairs because it's the biggest bank in this part of the country. It's got all the latest alarm systems.

KING. (*Crosses to divan with* PETER.) You don't say. You must tell us all about it.

DOC. (*Joins them at divan. Smoothly.*) Yeah. That's one bank that couldn't be robbed, I guess, huh?

PETER. Of course it could! It must have a weak link somewhere.

[1] Copyright, 1938, 1940, by Allan Wood.

KING. Of course!

PETER. I was keeping our money in my trunk under the bed. I had it connected to the electric lights in case of burglars, but my landlady was looking for some lost towels and almost got electrocuted.

KING. And you put your money in the bank downstairs without analyzing it? Do you think that was wise?

PETER. Gale wouldn't let me. She knew I'd find the weak link, then we'd worry. Mr. Garvey, the cashier, lives in South Liverpool. He's home sick with arthritis. When he told us that inside the vault they have an electric eye that gives the alarm the instant a ray of light strikes it, well—I felt better.

DOC. (*Stunned.*) An electric—then—no burglar could open that vault with a torch?

KING. An acetylene flame.

PETER. Oh! Never! That would be the quickest way to sound an alarm.

DOC. That sinks us.

PETER. What?

KING. Nothing. Yet you think it could be done? Some way that bank could be robbed safely—

PETER. Robbed safely?

KING. (*Hastily.*) For the burglar, I mean.

PETER. Of course! But I won't let my mind dwell on it, or I won't sleep tonight. I never had a hundred dollars before, at one time, I mean. Most of it was Gale's. When we get five hundred we're going to be married.

KING. Look, Peter— Every week the steel-mill payroll is in the vault downstairs over the week-end. It comes in on the train from Cleveland—and a hundred thousand dollars!

PETER. (*Impressed.*) A hundred thousand dollars? Maybe I should have gone to the steel mill. (*He rises and crosses to window.*) They ought to be very interested if I analyzed the bank and showed them how their payroll could be stolen.

KING. (*Follows to right of desk.*) No, no! You came to the right place. No one could be more interested than we are.

DOC. (*Crossing front of desk.*) That's absolutely right. All we care about in this world is to see that that money gets into the right hands—and maybe you're the boy to help us.

PETER. (*Behind desk and overcome at so much attention.*) You're very kind. Now—er—about salary?

KING. Oh, yes. Of course we will want you to be satisfied, and you're thinking of getting married, so we must—shall we say —a hundred? To start?

PETER. (*He can't believe his own ears.*) A hundred? A month? Wonderful—

KING. A week—!

PETER. (*Sitting behind desk.*) A week?

KING. You caught that fellow last night in Marshall's jewelry store— We want to do something for you for that.

DOC. Oh, we must do something for you for that!

PETER. But a hundred dollars a week—gosh! Catching that burglar was nothing, really.

DOC. To you, perhaps, but you don't know how much it meant to us. We're going to see that you get everything that's coming to you. Aren't we, Mr. King?

KING. And how!

PETER. (*Rises and crosses to* DOC.) Oh, you don't know what this is going to mean for me.

DOC. Oh, yes, we do. Better than you do—

PETER. But you can't— I—I—I'll never live long enough to be able to thank you.

KING. (*Crossing left of* PETER.) I believe you've got something there, Mason.

DOC. Yes! You hit the nail right on the head that time.

MARCH HARES [1]

by

HARRY WAGSTAFF GRIBBLE

At first glance GEOFFREY *appears to be merely an unusually attractive young man. On knowing him, one realizes that he is mentally extraordinary as well.* FULLER *is a more normal person. And yet, we could wish all "normal" people were as well-groomed, intelligent and gentle.*

FULLER. Well, I'll slip along.

GEOFFREY. No, no. I'm wide awake. (*He motions him to a chair by the couch.*) And I should be so much obliged if you would talk me to sleep.

FULLER. What shall I say?

GEOFFREY. Ask me questions. They always make me sleepy.

FULLER. (*Sitting.*) Very well. Why did you invite me?

GEOFFREY. Because I was furious at Janet.

FULLER. What about?

GEOFFREY. Because she was going to bring the Kitts girl here.

FULLER. Did you want me to carry off Miss Kitts?

GEOFFREY. I never thought of that. It's a brilliant idea, though. Do you think you could?

FULLER. I think anyone could, if he set his mind on it.

GEOFFREY. Well, we'll talk about that later. It was awfully nice of you to come here.

FULLER. I am always looking for adventure.

GEOFFREY. Oh. What does that mean?

FULLER. Look it up in Webster.

GEOFFREY. Oh, my God! The way people puzzle me!

FULLER. Why do men go to foreign countries?

GEOFFREY. Because they are sick of their own. Is that the right answer?

FULLER. There is another one.

GEOFFREY. Yes. Go on.

FULLER. Exploration.

GEOFFREY. Oh, yes. And what did you want to explore here?

FULLER. This foreign country in which you live.

GEOFFREY. It is like a foreign country, isn't it? I often think that myself. And I am like an Aborigine—or a Hottentot—or an Aztec—am I not?

FULLER. Quite like an Aztec—a remnant of an ancient and brilliant civilization.

GEOFFREY. I don't care about the "remnant" at all. I do feel "ancient." I know I am not "brilliant," and I find it impossible to be "civilized," so I feel that you couldn't have described me worse. But still, I am glad I appear odd to you, and I should like to be interesting. I wonder what you really are. Are you a gentleman at large, or have you some business? You aren't a detective, I know. No detective ever studied elocution.

FULLER. I told you. I am an explorer. I like the unusual. Your invitation was very unusual. You are so unusual yourself, that I felt sure your surroundings would be. They certainly are.

GEOFFREY. I see. And now you can go back and make notes about it all.

FULLER. I am making mental notes now.

GEOFFREY. About me?

FULLER. Yes.

GEOFFREY. I am sure they would horrify me.

FULLER. I hardly think so.

GEOFFREY. You don't think I am insane, do you?

FULLER. No. You are the sanest man in the world. You strike a pose of insanity to cover your sensitiveness.

GEOFFREY. Yes, I am sensitive.

FULLER. By the way, did you give Mrs. Rodney the impression that I am in financial straits?

GEOFFREY. I—I—don't think— I don't know— Why?

FULLER. Because she didn't like to accept forty-one cents from me. She hinted that I must have a very small income—and she said that you "had told her"—but she wouldn't say what you had told.

GEOFFREY. (*Springing off the couch.*) I must straighten this out at once. I shall fetch her downstairs.

GOOD-BYE, MR. CHIPS [1]

by

JAMES HILTON AND BARBARA BURNHAM

To the Brookfield School MR. CHIPPING *came as a young man of twenty. He has endeared himself to his pupils largely through his quiet sense of humor.* SIR RICHARD COLLEY, *jolly, red-faced, is genuinely fond of* CHIPS.

COLLEY. Hullo . . . hullo! Hullo!

CHIPS. Colley, my dear boy!

COLLEY. Chips, old man . . . how are you? Been trying to find you everywhere. . . . (*They shake hands.*) Well! Well! Well! Well! Well! Still wearing the same old gown? Glad you haven't discarded that, Chips. We should all miss that gown, you know! (*Drops his voice.*) I say, what's this rumour I hear about you and Ralston having a row?

CHIPS. A rumour! Already?

COLLEY. My dear old boy, I only arrived at the school five minutes ago—late for the Governors' meeting y'know—and my own nephew rushes up to me in the quad, with some cock-and-bull yarn about you and Ralston. Goodness knows where he got it from!

CHIPS. I can guess where Vick got it from! Little devils!

COLLEY. Never mind that! The point is, is it true?

CHIPS. Yes, it's true. The Head's just been giving me—er—

a piece of his mind, Colley. I didn't much like it, I must confess.

COLLEY. A piece of his mind!

CHIPS. Colley, a few minutes ago, in this room, I had quite a shock. It oughtn't to have been a shock, perhaps, but still it was; and I wasn't prepared for it. I've got over it now, Colley; I can even see the Head's point of view. But I see mine, too; and I don't know yet, Colley, who is right. That's what's bothering me, now.

COLLEY. What the devil are you talking about?

CHIPS. He asked me to resign, Colley.

COLLEY. What? Ralston asked you to resign?

CHIPS. Yes. Do you think I should? I'm fifty-four, Colley, and I don't feel old at all. But Ralston thinks that I am. He may have been right, Colley. Perhaps I have grown old without noticing it.

COLLEY. Old! Why, man, what utter rubbish! Aren't we all as old as we feel? He's no right to talk to you like this. As Chairman of the Governors, Chips, I can tell you—we don't particularly care for Master Ralston. But you, Chips, why, Brookfield wouldn't be Brookfield without you, and we all know it.

CHIPS. Colley, my dear boy! Colley, you are quite sure? The school still needs me, you mean?

COLLEY. Do I not! Why, you are Brookfield, Chips. Grr—the impossible bounder. . . . Come on out and get a breath of fresh air, Chips. You look pale.

CHIPS. Ralston asked me to stay. He'll be back any minute.

COLLEY. Well, if he starts chucking his weight about again, tell him as politely as you like he can go to the devil.

CHIPS. He's coming back to hear my decision, about resigning, you know.

COLLEY. Is he, by Jove! Then I'll wait, too. And he shall get it from both of us. Why, damme, you can stay here till you're a hundred, if you feel equal to it. I only hope you do.

NATIVE SON [1]

by

PAUL GREEN AND RICHARD WRIGHT

BIGGER *has been sentenced to die for the murder of a white girl. Although it is true that* BIGGER *committed the crime, the immediate events leading up to it have never been offered in defense for they would not be accepted.*

MAX. I want to understand you, get near to you, Bigger.
BIGGER. (*Almost whispering.*) Understand me. She said that —understand me— (*His voice dies out.*)
MAX. And she was trying to help you, wasn't she? (*Pause.*) Don't you know she was trying to help you?
BIGGER. She made me feel like a dog! Yeah, that's the way all of 'em made me feel. In their big house I was all trembling and afraid. (*His voice trails off again.*)
MAX. (*Suddenly.*) Didn't you ever love anybody, Bigger?
BIGGER. Maybe I loved my daddy. Long time ago. They killed him. (*Suddenly shouting as he springs up and begins to pace the cell.*) . . . There you start again. You mix me all up! (*With a wild moan.*) You make me feel something could happen—something good maybe— (*Frenziedly.*) You creep in on me, crowd me to the wall, smother me and I want my breath, right up till that lightning hits me. Go away, Mr. Max.
MAX. That day I said we had made you what you were, a killer—maybe I was wrong—I want to know I was wrong— (*He gazes at* BIGGER *with white, pained face.*)
BIGGER. (*Softly, half to himself.*) His po' face like the face of Jesus hanging on that wall—like her face too.

[1] Copyright, 1940 (in novel form), by Richard Wright. Copyright, 1941 (in unpublished form), by Paul Green and Richard Wright. Copyright, 1941, by Paul Green and Richard Wright. Reprinted by permission of Harper & Brothers (for the U.S.A.) and The Musson Book Co., Ltd. (for Canada).

MAX. You killed Clara. Why? She loved you, she was good. You say you killed her.

BIGGER. (*Stopping his pacing.*) Yah, I killed her—

MAX. You're not crazy, and there's not that kind of crazy logic in this world. I ask you and all the time you say, "I just did." That's not it, not it.

BIGGER. Then I didn't kill her. They said I shot her. I didn't. Wasn't no use talking 'bout it. She didn't count. I just let 'em say it.

MAX. (*An uncertain joy in his voice.*) You didn't shoot her?

BIGGER. One their bullets went clean through her. I had her in my arms, I let her fall down—

MAX. (*With a shout.*) We could have proved it. I might have— Thank God. (*He sinks down on the cot, staring at* BIGGER.)

BIGGER. But I killed her just the same. All the time I'd been killing her the way I'd been killing myself. She suffered for me, followed me, and I didn't want it—wanted to be free to walk wild and free with steps a mile long over the houses, over the rivers, and straddling the mountains and on—something in me—

MAX. And you didn't want to be hindered—you'd kill anything that got in your way—

BIGGER. Reckon so. But I wasn't thinking of that then.

MAX. (*Watching him.*) And would you kill again, Bigger, if you could?

BIGGER. (*Quieting down.*) I dunno— Naw— Yessuh, I dunno. Sometimes I feel like it. Maybe you're wrong now and I am bad and rotten the way you thought at the trial—made bad, and like that other man said. I dunno what I am—got no way to prove it. (*Wetting his lips.*) All the time I lie here thinking, beating my head against the wall, trying to see through, over it, but can't. Maybe 'cause I'm gonna die makes me want to see—know what I am maybe. How can I die like that, Mr. Max?

MAX. If we knew how to live, Bigger, we'd know how to die.

BIGGER. Yeh, people can live together but a man got to die by himself. That don't make sense— He needs something to die by more than to live by.

THROUGH THE NIGHT [1]

by

Florence Ryerson and Colin Clements

DWIGHT HOLBROOK *is a well set-up man in his late fifties. He has always been affluent but the accounting of his money has been without due care. Some years ago he met a down and out* DRISCOLL, *liked him and appointed him his financial advisor. He does not suspect* DRISCOLL *of stealing the missing bonds.*

DRISCOLL. I believe I'll have another.

HOLBROOK. Help yourself.

DRISCOLL. Take one with me? (*As* HOLBROOK *starts to refuse.*) Oh, come on. Brace yourself for the wedding tomorrow.

HOLBROOK. (*Laughing.*) All right. (*As* DRISCOLL *picks up his glass.*) Not too much soda. And go on with your theory . . . I'm breathless. (*He goes back to his stamp book.* DRISCOLL *starts pouring and mixing the drinks. His back is to the desk as he does so, cutting off the view of the glasses from* HOLBROOK, *but not from the audience.*)

DRISCOLL. Well . . . suppose I found out, unexpectedly— (*He has some trouble getting the cork out of the whiskey bottle. He takes up the paper knife and pries it up.*)—that you had discovered the loss of the bonds and intended telling the police about it tomorrow morning. It's obvious I'd have to get ahead of you by doing something to stop you tonight. Now what would I do?

HOLBROOK. (*Mildly.*) *You're* telling *me!*

DRISCOLL. (*As though thinking it out, reaches into his breast pocket and brings out his handkerchief.*) Well, for one thing, I might slip some chloral hydrate into your drink. (*He glances toward* HOLBROOK, *sees he is rummaging in a desk drawer with his back half turned, and takes two capsules from his handkerchief.*)

HOLBROOK. And it might not work. Chloral is all right for putting you to sleep . . . but I believe the chances of its killing you are less than one to five. (*As he talks, we see that* DRISCOLL *has broken the capsules and is dropping their contents into one of the drinks.*) Take my advice, Mr. X, and use strychnine.

DRISCOLL. It's too easy to detect. (*He adds the soda water, then hands the drink to* HOLBROOK, *who takes it and crosses to chair at left.*) There you are. And the object of the chloral would not be to kill.

HOLBROOK. (*Smiling as he sits down.*) I'm disappointed. I thought this was going to be a murder.

DRISCOLL. It is—but not an ordinary murder. (*He picks up his own glass.*) You see, I wouldn't be planning to run away. I'd want to stay right here in the house, without being suspected.

HOLBROOK. In the case of a murder, everyone in the house would be suspected.

DRISCOLL. Not if I supplied a fall guy from outside.

HOLBROOK. Such as?

DRISCOLL. Such as—the Owl.

HOLBROOK. (*Chuckling.*) Rather neat!

DRISCOLL. I think so. They're watching for him, anyway. Smith's right in the house. What's to keep me from feeding you a shot of chloral in your drink. We *did* agree it had chloral in it, didn't we?

HOLBROOK. (*Chuckling.*) Yes. I held out for strychnine; but, if you like, we'll make it chloral. (*He takes a drink.*) No. I don't think I *do* like this brand as well as the last. Remind me to tell Bunny. Well, go on. . . . What would you do next?

DRISCOLL. I suppose I'd have to make conversation until you began to nod. That ought to be pretty soon. Chloral doesn't take long to act, does it?

HOLBROOK. Not with me. I've used it for headaches. But Mr. X wouldn't be likely to know that.

DRISCOLL. He might—if he were Bunny. He might even know where you keep your chloral.

HOLBROOK. Everyone in the house knows. It's in the hall medicine closet. (*He takes another long drink, and studies his glass.*) No, this isn't nearly so good as the last. (*Impatiently.*) All right— I'm knocked out by the chloral— Then what?

DRISCOLL. Then it would be a simple matter to lead you over to the window, lay you down, and finish you off permanently with—(*He turns, looks over the desk as though searching for a weapon.*) Suppose we say, those scissors. They're good and sharp.

HOLBROOK. (*Finishing his drink.*) The paper knife is sharper.

DRISCOLL. I've thought of that. But I handled the paper knife earlier in the evening, and again, just now. It might have finger-prints.

HOLBROOK. You'd be handling the scissors. Bound to, if you used them to commit murder.

DRISCOLL. But there wouldn't be any finger-prints. I'd be wearing gloves.

HOLBROOK. (*Passing his hand over his eyes, as though he is dizzy.*) Oh, yes, of course. They always wear gloves. (*He crosses to the desk, holds on to it, and slowly drops into the desk chair.*)

DRISCOLL. You see, I've thought of everything. *Everything.* Down to the last detail. That's where most murderers go wrong. No imagination. (*He looks at* HOLBROOK, *who is shaking his head as though to waken himself.*) What's the matter? Headache?

HOLBROOK. No; just sleepy. (*Looking at his watch, groggily.*) It *is* late. Better be getting to bed. (*He starts to rise; sits down.*) Funny, I feel dizzy. You must have made that stronger—(*His hand goes to his head again; he speaks thickly.*)—than usual. Much . . . stronger. (*He makes another attempt to rise. During this action,* DRISCOLL *has turned away, taken a pair of gray gloves from his pocket, and is putting them on.*) Afraid . . . I'll . . . have . . . to . . . ask you help me. (DRISCOLL *does not answer. With some difficulty,* HOLBROOK *turns and looks at him, sees the gloves, blinks stupidly.*) What—what are you— (*Suddenly a horrible thought breaks through his drugged brain. His eyes widen; he half draws himself up.*) You!

DRISCOLL. (*Smiling at him.*) Yes.

HOLBROOK. (*Trying to reach for his gun.*) No! Help! Somebody . . . help . . . me! (DRISCOLL *pushes him back into his chair.*)

DRISCOLL. It won't do any good to call. (*He puts his hand over* HOLBROOK's *mouth.*) There's no one to hear you. (*Under the pressure of* DRISCOLL's *strong hands,* HOLBROOK *slumps forward to the floor in front of the French windows, where he is concealed by the desk and chair.* DRISCOLL *looks down at him for a moment, then reaches toward the scissors on the desk . . . draws them from their case and bends over. He disappears for a moment behind the desk; when he rises, he is no longer holding the scissors. The glove on his right hand is apparently blood-stained, for he looks at the palm, worried. He draws something from his pocket, shakes it out. It is a mask, crudely cut out of a linen handkerchief. He bends over the body, but we cannot see what he is doing with the mask. Still working quickly, he opens the curtains a little, turns the key in the French window behind the desk, and opens it. He takes the pad from the desk chair, holds it on the outside of the windowpane nearest the lock, and strikes the pane a smart blow. There is the sound of one or two pieces of glass falling on the bricks of the terrace. He gives a muttered "damn," listens. Nothing happens. He goes on, with constantly increasing speed. He takes the pieces of broken glass from the pad and carefully arranges them on the floor inside the room, then puts the pad back on the desk chair. He moves over to the tray, picks up the glass he filled for* HOL-

BROOK *and wipes the finger-prints off with his handkerchief. He removes his gloves, rolls them into a ball, looks around quickly, decides to hide them in a wall flowerpot, then changes his mind and conceals them in the lower part of Aunt Loretta's gilt clock. He crosses toward the right, thinks of something, stops, draws the pearls from his pocket, goes back toward the center door, and deliberately throws them into the library. He retraces his steps, surveys the room for a moment, then nods his head, satisfied. He unlocks the hall door, opens it, and stands, half in the hall, looking back toward the library door. He uses his normal tone, slightly raised, as though speaking to someone in the inner room.)* See you in the morning. (*He takes a step into the hall, then comes back, as though recalled.*) What's that? (*Pauses, as though listening.*) No. No golf. You're forgetting we have a wedding on our hands! I'll take you on the next day. (*He laughs.*) All right . . . no handicap! I'm too sleepy to argue. Goodnight. (*He closes the door behind him.*)

FOR ONE MAN AND ONE WOMAN

SKYLARK [1]

by

SAMSON RAPHAELSON

LYDIA and TONY renounce the life of big business deals and dull dinner parties to take the long promised trip.

LYDIA. What do you suppose is the matter with them?

TONY. Well, they came here to feel sorry for us because I'm out of a job.

LYDIA. And then they found we're sorry for them because they have a job—and they couldn't take it!

TONY. I guess that's it.

LYDIA. Oh, Tony, I'm frightened. Everything is too perfect. I go round frightened to death that it won't last. And when I look at the faces of people on the streets, I feel ashamed of myself for being so lucky. . . . Aren't I an idiot—I'm crying!

TONY. Don't—or you'll have me crying, too. I feel pretty good myself.

LYDIA. (*Clinging to him.*) Oh, darling, let's be careful—be careful not to get killed by slipping in the bathtub. And when you cross the street—ask the policeman to help you!

TONY. I promise.

LYDIA. Tony . . .

TONY. Yes, dear?

LYDIA. I hate to sell the house.

TONY. I thought you wanted to sell it.

LYDIA. That was before somebody wanted to buy it.

73

TONY. (*Excited.*) Have we really got a customer?

LYDIA. The people who looked at it Friday. They came again this morning—I've been with them until now.

TONY. Well, I think that's great—don't you?

LYDIA. I don't know. . . .

TONY. But, darling—this is our chance to take that trip.

LYDIA. When I think of the house going into the hands of strangers . . . I put a lot of work into this house. . . . Oh, I'll be all right in a minute. . . .

TONY. (*Understandingly.*) Sure you will. (*Changing the subject to cheer her up.*) That's a new hairdress, isn't it?

LYDIA. Like it?

TONY. I love it. And your eyes are a new color, aren't they?

LYDIA. (*Brightening.*) I had them tinted a little to match the dress.

TONY. Darn sensible of you, too. (*She takes a cigarette, lights a match.* TONY *stops her hand.*)

TONY. Now make up your mind: are we going away, or aren't we?

LYDIA. I suppose we are.

TONY. Good. (*He lets her light the cigarette.*) Then we sell the house. That's that. You'll get over it in a week.

LYDIA. Thank you, darling! I needed someone to bully me. I feel better now.—Good-bye, windows! Good-bye, chairs! Good-bye, stairway!

TONY. Now don't get sentimental.

LYDIA. (*To the whole house.*) Good-bye—and nuts to you!

TONY. That's more like it.

TONY DRAWS A HORSE [1]

by

LESLEY STORM

MRS. PARSONS *is a sweetly aggressive type of person. She may rule the Woman's Club but she cannot intimidate* GRANDPA.

MRS. PARSONS. Sit down somewhere, dear, and let me prepare my speech. (*She goes to the desk and sits.*)

GRANDPA. (*Going to her.*) What's the speech about?

MRS. PARSONS. Nothing. I just have to introduce Harland Morris and thank him afterwards.

GRANDPA. Who's he?

MRS. PARSONS. The novelist. He's giving a lecture to the members of the league on his tour in Palestine. He's just written a book about it. . . .

GRANDPA. He won't be coming here, will he?

MRS. PARSONS. Possibly. Afterwards. . . . I told Agnes to get a few of his books from the library so that they could be lying about. . . . Do you know if she remembered?

GRANDPA. (*Looking round and seeing them on the table behind the settee.*) Yes, she did. They're here. (*He picks them up.*)

MRS. PARSONS. Better take out the library labels. It looks more permanent.

GRANDPA. (*Tearing out the first label.*) I don't see what the fuss is about. I've never heard of him.

MRS. PARSONS. Perhaps not, dear, but don't show your ignorance. And if he should come here, don't say you never read books.

GRANDPA. What'll I say I read?

MRS. PARSONS. Keep off the subject. If he does mention his

own books you can always say you think they're penetrating.

GRANDPA. Penetrating what?

MRS. PARSONS. It doesn't matter, dear. It's just a word one uses about books. (MRS. PARSONS *writes busily.* GRANDPA *puts the first book on the table behind the settee, tears out the label from the second book and puts it on the wireless set up left, and then, tearing out the third label as he crosses bangs the book down noisily on the desk. He then moves aimlessly round to the right of* MRS. PARSONS.) Did you want to say something, dear?

GRANDPA. I don't like using words I don't see the sense of.

MRS. PARSONS. Say they're sincere, then—or—sensitive— (*Airily.*) Anything non-committal. (*She writes for a moment and he moves near her. Looking up.*) If you do sit up, dear, will you wear your velvet jacket and cap?

GRANDPA. What for?

MRS. PARSONS. It looks very nice to see an old gentleman in a velvet jacket. It gives him an air.

GRANDPA. I don't mind the jacket so much. But I won't wear that fez.

MRS. PARSONS. It isn't a fez, dear. It's a smoking-cap.

GRANDPA. I think it's a bloody awful cap. I'd rather go to bed.

MRS. PARSONS. Please yourself, of course, dear. . . . Do you mind not talking while I try to concentrate?

GRANDPA. It's you that's doing all the talking. . . . Where's the evening paper?

MRS. PARSONS. (*Handing him the paper she has brought in.*) Here it is.

GRANDPA. I just want to see if there's any more news of that torso. (*He sits in the armchair by the fireplace.*)

MRS. PARSONS. Read the events in Europe, Father. Better for you than morbid mysteries.

GRANDPA. There's events in Europe every day. It isn't always there's a party found in a trunk.

MRS. PARSONS. Person.

GRANDPA. You can't call a torso a person.

MRS. PARSONS. You can't call it a party.

GRANDPA. I've worked it all out by the numerals from the time it was found—seven o'clock in the morning on the seventeenth of May. . . . And you know there's nothing to go by. No clues. No identifications.

MRS. PARSONS. I've never heard anything about it. Where was it found?

GRANDPA. In a trunk at Waterloo.

MRS. PARSONS. By your calculations it will probably turn out to be Napoleon. (*She enjoys her little joke.*)

CYPRIENNE [1]

by

MARGARET MAYO

DES PRUNELLES *realizing that he is about to lose his beautiful young wife decides that his only hope of holding her is to facilitate the divorce plans.* CYPRIENNE *is amazed at this side of her husband which she has never seen.*

DES PRUNELLES. (*Crosses to center table for his coat and hat, which* BASTIEN *has brought in. He turns to* CYPRIENNE, *who comes down stage.*) Good night, my dear.

CYPRIENNE. (*Stops in astonishment.*) Good night? We haven't dined yet.

DES PRUNELLES. I'm dining out, my child.

CYPRIENNE. But you can't—you've asked Adhemar here.

DES PRUNELLES. To dine with you, my dear—not with me.

CYPRIENNE. I won't have it! I wish you to be here.

DES PRUNELLES. (*Affecting surprise.*) What?

CYPRIENNE. It's more fun when there are three.

DES PRUNELLES. It's sweet of you, my dear, not to make me feel in the way, but I couldn't think of intruding. It would embarrass the boy—and annoy him.

CYPRIENNE. I'd like to stir up some sort of human emotion in him.

DES PRUNELLES. Are you speaking of the ardent Adhemar?

CYPRIENNE. Ardent? Since he's made up his mind to marry me, he's—he's a stuffed mummy.

DES PRUNELLES. I'm sorry, my dear, but I'm afraid I must go. You see, I've made other arrangements, and—

CYPRIENNE. You wish to go?

DES PRUNELLES. (*Apologetically.*) After all, Cyprienne, it's a long time since I've been a bachelor and had my fling, and—

CYPRIENNE. (*Pouts.*) You've spoiled my whole evening. (*Pleads.*) Please stay.

DES PRUNELLES. But I've promised.

CYPRIENNE. (*Comes to him and takes his hand.*) Promised? Promised whom? Where are you dining?

DES PRUNELLES. At the Café Grand Vatel.

CYPRIENNE. (*Suspiciously.*) Alone?

DES PRUNELLES. Well— (*He takes his hand away.*) That is—

CYPRIENNE. I don't believe you.

DES PRUNELLES. Cyprienne!

CYPRIENNE. There is someone waiting for you. You said yourself you'd promised.

DES PRUNELLES. A slip of the tongue.

CYPRIENNE. It's a woman.

DES PRUNELLES. (*Laughs.*) But, Cyprienne—

CYPRIENNE. Why don't you own up—you're going to meet some woman. . . . Who is it?

DES PRUNELLES. You said you didn't care.

CYPRIENNE. I don't care—only I want to know.

DES PRUNELLES. But why?

CYPRIENNE. Is she young?

DES PRUNELLES. She's not ancient.

CYPRIENNE. It's perfectly ridiculous for a man of your age to marry a young woman. Is she pretty—is she prettier than I?

DES PRUNELLES. Impossible, my dear.

CYPRIENNE. (*Half crying.*) I wish you wouldn't joke. I don't think it's funny.

DES PRUNELLES. I beg your pardon, Cyprienne.

CYPRIENNE. I'm disappointed in you. The idea of you running about after some chit of a girl the moment I'm through with you. It's ridiculous—it infuriates me!

DES PRUNELLES. (*Laughs.*) I'm sorry, my dear.

CYPRIENNE. You're not, and your levity is disgusting. It's an insult. You've been grinning from ear to ear ever since we discussed divorce. I've never seen you so happy.

DES PRUNELLES. (*Takes her hand.*) You wouldn't have me scowling, would you? And making selfish objections. I'm happy to see you happy. (*Draws her to him and strokes her hair.*) And you are happy, aren't you, dear?

CYPRIENNE. (*Kneeling on armchair right of center table and sniffling.*) Ye-s.

DES PRUNELLES. What more can you ask?

CYPRIENNE. (*About to cry.*) I want you—to be sorry—to lose— (*Tumbles into his arms sobbing.*)

DES PRUNELLES. My child!

CYPRIENNE. (*Crying.*) You throw me away—like an old bouquet.

DES PRUNELLES. (*Holds her in his arms.*) You wanted to separate—

CYPRIENNE. With regrets. I have regrets—you haven't a single one. And we've been so happy together—sometimes—haven't we, Henri?

DES PRUNELLES. Sometimes.

CYPRIENNE. Very often; you know we have. I haven't forgotten, if you have.

DES PRUNELLES. (*Kisses the hair on her forehead.*) My big baby!

CYPRIENNE. (*Coaxing.*) You will dine with me tonight—won't you, Henri? Ah, say you will. Just this once. It may be our last time together. You can dine with the other—thing—tomorrow.

DES PRUNELLES. But there is no other.

CYPRIENNE. You're beginning again.

DES PRUNELLES. Shall I prove it to you?

CYPRIENNE. (*Joyfully.*) Can you?

DES PRUNELLES. Nothing easier.

CYPRIENNE. But how?

DES PRUNELLES. You shall dine with me yourself.

CYPRIENNE. At the Café Grand Vatel?

DES PRUNELLES. Just we two together.

CYPRIENNE. Oh, you darling!

DES PRUNELLES. You'll come?

CYPRIENNE. (*Laughs and crosses left for hat.*) At least I'll know that you are not dining with any other woman. Where's my coat? Here you are, get me in it. (*Hands coat to* DES PRUNELLES, *who holds it for her.*)

DES PRUNELLES. What a pretty coat! (*Puts it around her shoulders and kisses back of her neck.*)

CYPRIENNE. (*Pleased.*) Henri!

DES PRUNELLES. Good Heavens! I'd forgotten.

CYPRIENNE. What?

DES PRUNELLES. Adhemar! It's not loyal.

CYPRIENNE. (*Amazed.*) Stop it! Drop it!

DES PRUNELLES. We'll have to take him with us.

CYPRIENNE. Oh, bother Adhemar! I'll have to dine with him for the rest of my life.

DES PRUNELLES. He'll be angry.

CYPRIENNE. So much the better.

DES PRUNELLES. He'll make a scene.

CYPRIENNE. I can't help that. Anyway, I couldn't dine alone with Adhemar. It wouldn't be decent. (*Puts finishing touches to make up from vanity case.*)

DES PRUNELLES. With your future husband?

CYPRIENNE. The servants can't know that. And besides, I'm bored to death at the thought of him. I'm going to dine with you—just we two. (*Takes his arm.*)

DES PRUNELLES. As you say, my dear.

THIS THING CALLED LOVE [1]

by

EDWIN BURKE

ANN *is a modern well-poised young woman. The Sheriff has taken the name of her tearoom, The Dew Drop Inn, literally.* TICE COLLINS *has returned from Peru after a prolonged absence from this country.*

ANN. (*Left of couch right.*) I'm frightfully ashamed.

COLLINS. That's what you meant by digging for motives.

ANN. Yes. You mustn't think me heartless, but—while I wouldn't have had this happen for anything, since it did, I am glad. They'll be divorced now. That will, at least, keep them from going insane.

COLLINS. (*Looking at her.*) Is that what keeps you from getting married?

ANN. I've seen so much of it. My mother and father—mad about each other—couldn't get along. I think it hastened my mother's death.

COLLINS. Why don't you marry me?

ANN. You'd still go through with it after what you've just seen?

COLLINS. That'd never happen to me.

ANN. (*Admiringly.*) Well, you're no coward.

COLLINS. Will you?

ANN. No, thanks. (*Crosses to fireplace.*)

COLLINS. Well, you can't say that I don't try. Aren't you ever going to get married?

ANN. Not as marriage is today. Of course, old standards are changing. Some one may work out a new system, discover a sounder basis. I may try it then.

COLLINS. (*Smilingly.*) I hope I'm around.

[1] Copyright, 1928, by Edwin Burke (under the title of "Bed and Board"). Copyright, 1929, by Samuel French.

ANN. (*Smilingly.*) I promise to get in touch with you immediately.

COLLINS. (*A new thought.*) Did your sister really mean that Miss Alvaraz had a position with Russell & Co.?

ANN. Yes.

COLLINS. An official position?

ANN. I think she's the Sex Appeal. (*Sits on chair down left.*) You see, women are employed as everything today.

COLLINS. Yes, they— (*Suddenly.*) Say, why wouldn't it be a good idea for a man to employ a woman as his wife?

ANN. (*Smilingly.*) Now, there's the solution. In the event she proved unsatisfactory, the husband needn't bother about a divorce.

COLLINS. And if she didn't like the job she could quit.

ANN. Lovely. Fancy a woman saying to her husband, "I'm leaving the first of the month. You'll have to get another wife." (*They both laugh.*) Are you trying to solve the marriage problem?

COLLINS. You can't tell me there isn't some way to absolutely insure success. (*Sits on taboret.*)

ANN. (*Rather seriously, after moment's thought.*) I know a way.

COLLINS. What?

ANN. Keep love out of it. Love with its two little playmates, selfishness and jealousy. That's what ruins most marriages. (*Stops suddenly; thinks a moment.*) Why don't— (*Continues to ponder.*)

COLLINS. (*After a pause.*) What?

ANN. (*After another thoughtful pause.*) You know, that idea of hiring a wife may not be as silly as it sounds.

COLLINS. Oh, I was just kidding.

ANN. (*Thoughtfully.*) I watched you very closely this evening. You were enthralled by the atmosphere of this lovely home. The music created a sentimental mood which the cocktails accentuated. I don't think I ever saw anyone so supremely contented. You wouldn't have surprised me had you started to purr.

COLLINS. I felt great.

ANN. But don't you see? You were being made happy by purely creative comforts that have nothing whatever to do with conjugal love. Any clever woman, experienced in the art of being a hostess, could bring about the same results. (*Suddenly*.) Are you a gambler?

COLLINS. Yes.

ANN. (*Decisively*.) So am I. And most of the important things in my life I've done on impulse. I have a hunch. If you want to hire a wife, I'd like the job.

COLLINS. I asked you to marry me.

ANN. I'm applying for a position.

COLLINS. You mean you'd really do it?

ANN. Why not? I have to make my own living. It has all the excitement of a gamble. If we win— how glorious! If we lose—well, we lose!

COLLINS. (*Enthusiastically*.) Come on. (*Rises*.)

ANN. Remember. It's only a job.

COLLINS. You mean you don't want to get married?

ANN. Oh, yes. I'd hardly have the courage not to get married—merely as a formality. For instance, I could see that you had a home as lovely as this. You could probably have this. They won't need it after tonight. I'd be the head of your household. I'd look after your physical comforts, entertain your friends, in short, you would have everything that a wealthy married man could have except wrangling and—Sex Appeal.

COLLINS. Oh! No Sex Appeal?

ANN. I'd have regular hours and I'd sleep home at night.

COLLINS. I don't like that "sleep home nights."

ANN. You could have your friends. If they happened to be ladies, that would be your business. If my friends happened to be gentlemen, that would be my business. I'm sure you wouldn't do anything to embarrass me. And, of course, I wouldn't do anything to embarrass you.

COLLINS. I'd have sort of a glorified housekeeper.

ANN. Actually. Yes. But so far as the public was concerned, you'd have the most loving and dutiful of wives.

COLLINS. (*Hesitantly.*) Well, er, ah, would you expect me to—ah—er—be faithful to you?

ANN. No. You could be just the average husband.

COLLINS. Suppose either of us fell in love with somebody?

ANN. We'd sign an agreement—that the moment the arrangement proved unsuitable to either of us, we'd be divorced. (COLLINS *becomes thoughtful.*)

ANN. We haven't talked salary.

COLLINS. You'd expect salary?

ANN. It's customary on the part of one taking a position.

COLLINS. No, I didn't mean it that way. All right. (*Falling into the spirit of it.*) Well, what is your salary? Think up a good one.

ANN. Twenty-five thousand dollars a year and all expenses—

COLLINS. That's a good one. (COLLINS *crosses right.*)

ANN. —except clothes. I'd buy my own. Salary stops the day either of us decides to call it off. You see, I'd never ask for alimony. The salary may seem large, but of course in these days you have to pay for service.

COLLINS. (*Heartily.*) The salary is great. I'm for it.

ANN. You really want to do it?

COLLINS. The sooner the better.

ANN. All right. Tomorrow morning.

COLLINS. Great! We'll be married in the morning.

HERE TODAY [1]

by

GEORGE OPPENHEIMER

CLAIRE *is the beautiful and spoiled darling of the aristocratic Windrew family. She is in love with* PHILIP GRAVES,

[1] Copyright, 1932, by George Oppenheimer. Copyright, 1940, by Samuel French.

a well known and carefree novelist. The scene of the romance is at Nassau, the Bahamas.

CLAIRE. (*Finally pushes him off.*) Dearest, you're choking me.

PHILIP. Then it was you I proposed to last night? There can't be two people so attractive.

CLAIRE. And it was you I accepted. Oh, Phil, I love you so much!

PHILIP. I'm afraid I'm pretty hopelessly in love with you. You know that, don't you?

CLAIRE. Oh, I hope so. Phil, why do you love me? I'm not really the kind of girl you ought to love.

PHILIP. Sorry. It's too late to do anything about that.

CLAIRE. Imagine getting engaged at the Casino—in a gambling house.

PHILIP. It's the first time I ever won anything in one of those places.

CLAIRE. Spencer was much more proper. He proposed to me in a conservatory.

PHILIP. Under a potted palm, with *his* mother on one side of it and *yours* on the other.

CLAIRE. (*Tenderly.*) Fool!

PHILIP. About you, anyway. (*They embrace.*)

CLAIRE. Oh, if there were only nobody to consider but ourselves. If Mother wasn't set on Spencer, and Spencer wasn't so—

PHILIP. Now don't start worrying again.

CLAIRE. I can't help it. I get cold shivers every time I think of breaking the news to Mother.

PHILIP. I don't suppose there is much to recommend me. I'm poor, I have no social connections, I drink like a fish—and I love it.

CLAIRE. (*Crosses to center.*) Phil, what am I going to tell her? Oh, I hope she'll like you.

PHILIP. Darling! To see me is to love me.

CLAIRE. And when I think of Spencer arriving here any minute— What time is it?

PHILIP. Oh, I don't know. About half past eleven.

CLAIRE. His plane lands at noon. I've got to meet him. That'll be nice. After all, Phil, here he is coming all the way to Nassau thinking he's engaged to me—and he is engaged to me. And then I tell him, "No, I've met another man." What's he going to do?

PHILIP. (*Sits on sofa.*) He's going to go home again.

CLAIRE. I wish it were as easy as that. Phil, you come from a sort of Bohemian crowd that doesn't take those things seriously, but Mother and Boston aren't like that. A broken engagement! It's just not done. And going outside her little group. Why, Mother knows only about seven families in Boston. Spencer's family dates back to the Flood.

PHILIP. Has there been a flood? I never see a paper down here.

CLAIRE. (*To left arm of sofa.*) And to think that I was once in love with him—or thought I was. It couldn't have been love. If I ever married him, I'd be doing the same dull things that I've done all my life—until I met you, darling. . . . I'm going to break away from it all! (*They kiss.*)

PHILIP. Darling, why can't we just elope? Run away and get married and then what can they do about it?

CLAIRE. Oh, Phil! We couldn't. Mother would never forgive me. And Spencer—it's bad enough to hurt him this way. No, Phil, if we do it at all, we've got to do it right with Mother's blessing and Spencer's forgiveness—

PHILIP. And eight thousand relations and tons of flat silver. Why don't they ever give curved silver? There's an interesting research problem.

CLAIRE. Oh, everything's so complicated.

THE PHILADELPHIA STORY [1]

by

P<small>HILIP</small> B<small>ARRY</small>

On the eve of her second marriage TRACY LORD *returns home from a party with her brother* SANDY. *They are conniving to suppress an article about the family that is being written and photographed by a nationally known magazine.*

SANDY. The question is, can we get away with it?

TRACY. You've got to get away with it! You must, Sandy!

SANDY. It's your idea, not mine.

TRACY. What difference does that make? (*She pours herself a glass of champagne.*)

SANDY. You get the ideas and I do all the work.

TRACY. Sandy!

SANDY. Okay.

TRACY. What you don't already know about the great Sidney Kidd, you can certainly fill in from Mike's ravings tonight.

SANDY. I used to have that Dime lingo down pretty pat.

TRACY. It's a chance to write a beauty: you know it is.

SANDY. Then I swap it with Kidd for Connor's piece on us —and where am I?

TRACY. You'll have the satisfaction of knowing you saved the lot of us single-handed.

SANDY. And if he won't swap?

TRACY. I'm not worried about that.

SANDY. I suppose there's a fair chance the *Post* would go for it.

TRACY. Of course! You can't possibly lose. Quick—they'll be here! How long will it take you?

SANDY. Three thousand words—all night—what there's left of it. (*He looks at his watch.*) Holy cats! You get to bed.

TRACY. Have you got a typewriter?

SANDY. My old Corona is upstairs, I think.

TRACY. Make it smoke.

SANDY. You bet.

TRACY. Suds. I can't stand it. You won't fall asleep?

SANDY. I've drunk nothing but black coffee since Connor began his lecture.

TRACY. "Sidney Kidd—his habits—his habitat—and how to hunt him."

SANDY. Poor Connor! It must have been bottled up in him for years.

TRACY. Waiter, another bottle.

SANDY. No. I've got enough for three articles now: profile, full-face—

TRACY. —Also rear elevation.—Mike and Liz—they mustn't suspect, Sandy.

SANDY. Oh, no—oh my, no!

TRACY. They have simply stepped in their own chewing gum.—I suppose Kidd has one of those private numbers the rich and the mighty hide behind in New York.

SANDY. I'll dig it out of Liz and give him a buzz.

TRACY. What will you say?

SANDY. I'll be brief, bluff, belligerent. (TRACY *laughs and pours herself another glass of champagne.*) Here—lay off that!

TRACY. Why?

SANDY. You are already in wine, sister.

TRACY. Me? You lie. It never affects me, not in the slightest.

SANDY. That's because you never take it.

MR. AND MRS. NORTH [1]

by

Owen Davis

MR. *and* MRS. NORTH *returned to their little apartment in Greenwich Village to find a dead man in their closet.*

8 P.M. to 9 P.M. that night. NORTH *on seat down right.*

PAM *on sofa right center. They have been eagerly reading all the late afternoon papers which are in evidence all about them.*

PAM. Oh dear! It's just simply too awful!

NORTH. (*Starts reading about the murder from another paper.*) I know!

PAM. When Mother reads these papers!

NORTH. I'm wondering what they'll say at the office!

PAM. Only one of these papers insinuated that you were the murderer.

NORTH. Nice thing—at my time of life— Here I am, a respectable, conservative, conventional—

PAM. Oh no! That's worse than a murderer!

NORTH. And nobody knows who the poor devil was, no identification!

PAM. Those detectives will identify him, all right.

NORTH. Of course—all I know about murder mysteries I learned from the books we've published—but we've published a lot better detectives than that!

PAM. Well, when Lieutenant Weigand comes I'm going to show them the clue I found, and I'm going to ask them to open that closet in Dorothy's room.

NORTH. Open Dorothy's closet? What for?

PAM. Well—

NORTH. (*Rises; crossing left center.*) You don't expect to find a dead man in every closet, do you?

PAM. I didn't expect to find one in there, did I? I'm sure Lieutenant Weigand will do it for me; he's really very nice, and not in the least what I would have expected.

NORTH. No? What would you have expected?

PAM. Well, he certainly shouldn't be just like anybody else, but he is. He smokes cigarettes and takes off his hat and everything!

NORTH. He's all right I expect, must be or they wouldn't have made him a Lieutenant. Pam—

PAM. He's nice, as a person, a little disappointing.

NORTH. (*Goes rather gravely to her as she reads the paper.*) Pam! About that compact—

PAM. Oh, Jerry—you're not going to start talking about that again, are you?

NORTH. (*Gravely.*) The compact we found under the table there, was not the one you gave to the Lieutenant.

PAM. (*Pretends surprise.*) Why, Jerry!

NORTH. You gave him a big black one, the one we found was gold.

PAM. (*Innocently.*) Are you sure, Jerry?

NORTH. I'm very sure. It was an old one of yours, I gave it to you myself.

PAM. You always do give me such lovely things!

NORTH. (*Sternly.*) Don't change the subject. You know perfectly well that was not the same compact, don't you? (*She turns away.*) You do. What will you do if that detective finds out the trick you played on him? Now I don't think you took it, but I think you know who did. Do you?

PAM. Well!

NORTH. Do you know?

PAM. I think I know—I'm not sure—not quite sure—but it didn't have anything to do with the murder, Jerry—and I don't want to tell you any more about it.

NORTH. Why don't you?

PAM. Because you couldn't keep it to yourself.

NORTH. Why couldn't I? (*Slips down on sofa.*)

PAM. Because you're not a woman.

NORTH. You aren't actually trying to tell me that women can keep a secret better than men can?

PAM. They can keep the ones they want to.

NORTH. (*Trying to win her over.*) Pam! You tell me this one.

PAM. This is one of the ones. Please, Jerry—it's just silly —not anything to make a fuss about, only the detectives think everything is a clue, and any talk about this might make a lot of trouble for a very good friend of ours.

NORTH. Gossip, you mean?

PAM. Yes, Jerry.

NORTH. Just gossip—you're sure?

PAM. Yes, dear. Now, please don't worry, as soon as they find out who that poor man was I'm sure they will be able to find out who murdered him, and why. We are all right, Jerry, Lieutenant Weigand practically said we were all right because we didn't even know the murdered man. (*The buzzer sounds and* NORTH *goes and pushes the ticker.*)

NORTH. Oh, I suppose so, only I'll be glad when this thing is all over.

PAM. I know, but in no time at all now, we'll be going to camp, then all you'll have to worry about will be the hunting.

NORTH. Let's go Friday, if the police will let us.

PAM. If I can get ready.

NORTH. The sooner we get out of this, the better!

PAM. But not until they find the murderer, we couldn't miss that—it's so exciting!

YES AND NO [1]

by

KENNETH HORNE

JO *carries an air of inconsequent vagueness—and moves with the exuberant uncontrol of a colt. In repose she is never in a normal position, either squatting or reclining.* BAGSHOTT *has a slight stammer. He is likable, kindly, and humorous.*

BAGSHOTT. (*Breaking the silence.*) Going to play tennis?

JO. (*Sadly.*) No!

BAGSHOTT. Why not?

JO. For one thing, it's too hot, and for another—I don't want to.

BAGSHOTT. Oh, it'll be cooler after tea and—

JO. (*Interrupting with slight asperity.*) I don't want to play tennis, and I don't want to talk about tennis.

BAGSHOTT. (*A little startled.*) You don't?

JO. No, I don't.

BAGSHOTT. Oh! . . . What on earth were you talking about just now? What stark tragedy? (JO *does not reply, but slowly crumples into a rather ungainly heap, with her face buried in her hands.* BAGSHOTT *looks at her anxiously and stops cutting. Suddenly her shoulders begin to shake, and* BAGSHOTT, *his face filled with concern, takes a step towards her. Staring uncertainly down at her.*) Jo! (*Much worried.*) Jo—what are you doing? (*He turns towards the French windows, as though to call back* MRS. JARROW, *and makes a mooing noise which is peculiar to him.*) Mmmm! (BAGSHOTT *goes down stage to right of* JO *and stands in agitation over her, not knowing how to deal with situation, owing to her awkward attitude.*) Jo—what's the matter? Are you crying or laughing? (JO *turns a distorted face up to him.*)

JO. (*Sobbing audibly.*) I—I'm not laughing.

BAGSHOTT. (*Greatly distressed.*) Good Lord, what is it? What's happened?—Don't do that, please. Please don't, Jo. (JO *mumbles something inaudible amidst her sobs.*) What? (JO *repeats the inaudible mumble. He puts the knife down on the table, and returns to her.*) I can't hear what you're saying down there. Do stand up. Stand up and tell me, Jo. Please! (JO, *with his help, struggles to her feet, and, immediately burying her face in his chest, breaks into a torrent of tears.* BAGSHOTT *puts an arm comfortingly around her. Gently.*) What's the trouble, little Jo?

JO. (*Sobbing.*) I can't bear it.

BAGSHOTT. What can't you bear?

JO. His eyes. His awful anguished eyes. (*She puts her arms round him.*)

BAGSHOTT. Whose eyes?

JO. (*Sobbing with less violence.*) Adrian's.

BAGSHOTT. What's the matter with them?

JO. (*Speaking into his chest.*) They haunt me. I shall see them for the rest of my life. Oh, Bags, I've never hurt anybody before.

BAGSHOTT. But how have you hurt him?

JO. I wouldn't marry him.

BAGSHOTT. (*In a relieved tone.*) Oh, is that all?

JO. (*Drawing a little away from him.*) Is that all! Well, I tell you—if anybody else ever asks me to marry them—I shall do it. I can't go through this again. (*She buries her face in his chest again.*)

BAGSHOTT. But you're quite right not to marry him if you don't love him..

JO. But how do I know I don't love him?

BAGSHOTT. (*With undue vehemence.*) Of course you don't.

JO. Why not?

BAGSHOTT. Well, it's—it's ridiculous. There's nothing about the man to attract a girl like you, for one thing.—And for another, you wouldn't have turned him down if you had.

JO. Wouldn't I?

BAGSHOTT. Of course not.

JO. Are you sure? (*She draws a little away.*)

BAGSHOTT. Absolutely certain.

JO. (*Doubtfully.*) All right, then. If you're sure. But what am I going to do about him? (*She puts her arms round him again.*)

BAGSHOTT. Nothing. Forget it.—Good Lord, you frightened me to death. I thought it was something serious.

JO. So it is serious. You'd know what it felt like if anybody had ever asked you.

BAGSHOTT. (*Slightly flippant.*) How do you know they haven't?

JO. (*Still sniffling.*) Because you're a man and you don't mix with the class of women who do that sort of thing.

BAGSHOTT. (*Laughing.*) Anyway, I don't think there's much wrong with his eyes.

JO. (*Draws away from him.*) Oh, that's only because you see them from the outside, but if you look into them, deep down into the depths of them—

BAGSHOTT. (*Flippantly.*) I doubt if he'd appreciate my doing that.

JO. (*Pleading tearfully.*) Oh, Bags, don't make fun of me.

BAGSHOTT. But I wasn't—

JO. Please don't make fun of me. It's so terribly serious.

BAGSHOTT. (*Immediately sympathetic.*) I'm not making fun of you, my sweet.

JO. Aren't you? (*She puts her arms round him.*)

BAGSHOTT. Of course not.

JO. And you're quite sure I don't love him?

BAGSHOTT. Positive!

THE MALE ANIMAL [1]

by

JAMES THURBER AND ELLIOTT NUGENT

TOMMY *and* ELLEN TURNER *have been living quietly and unobtrusively in a small university town for ten years. Comes the school's greatest football hero who was once very fond of* ELLEN. TOMMY, *harassed by academic difficulties, is losing his perspective.*

ELLEN. Tommy, (*She puts her hand on his shoulder.*) listen to me. . . . I wanted to have a good time last night, and you spoiled it. . . .

TOMMY. Didn't you enjoy it at all?

ELLEN. (*Piqued.*) Yes, I did. I'm not a hundred years old—yet. I just decided to quit worrying about you and have a little fun. For about an hour I felt like a girl again—wearing flowers at a Spring dance—when I was young and silly. . . .

TOMMY. Young and happy.

ELLEN. All right, he . . . kissed me. I kissed him, too. We didn't go out in the dark to do it.

TOMMY. (*Piling the books he is taking from the book-shelves on the settee.*) I hope you didn't lend that book to anybody; it was a first edition. . . . I wish we had had separate bookplates.

ELLEN. (*Beginning to flame.*) So that when you really make me mad and I get out of here, I can find my own books quickly?

TOMMY. I hate sentimental pawing over things by a couple breaking up. We're not living in the days of Henry James and Meredith. Look at Joe and his wife.

ELLEN. Tommy. (*She goes to him again.*) I want you to stop this. If you're going to be jealous be jealous, rave or throw things, but don't act like the lead in a senior-class play! (*This thrust gets home.*)

TOMMY. (*Angrily.*) I'm trying to tell you that I don't care what you and Joe do! I'm trying to tell you that it's fine! It's very lucky that he came back just now.

ELLEN. Why, what do you mean?

TOMMY. I mean on the money I make, I can go on fine alone, reading whatever I want to to my classes! That's what I want! And that's what I'm going to do. . . .

ELLEN. (*Full of exclamation points.*) So that's why you've been wandering around! That's what you've been figuring out! How nice it would be if he would take me off your hands, so you could be left alone with your books and match boxes and litter! I suppose any man would do as well as Joe! (*She rushes up to him.*)

TOMMY. (*Rising to face her.*) He's not just any man, and you know that! He's always been in love with you, and you've always been in love with him! (*He is angry and jealous now and brings up his own exclamation points.*)

ELLEN. That's ridiculous! . . . (*Worried, angry and tired.*) All right—have it your way. If you want to be free, then I want to be free—and I've gone around for ten years mooning about Joe. . . . Well, maybe I have—maybe I have, because I'm certainly sick of you right now! (*She whirls away from him.*)

NO TIME FOR COMEDY [1]

by

S. N. BEHRMAN

The lovely LINDA—*clever, sane and glamorous—is one of the "important" actresses. Her husband,* GAYLORD EASTER-

BROOK, *is an established playwright. Between engagements, both are nervous and unhappy.*

GAY. Let's go out for dinner.

LINDA. (*A slight hesitation.*) I've made a dinner date.

GAY. (*Another moment.*) Oh—have you?

LINDA. I had no way of knowing whether you were coming home or not—I didn't feel in the mood of eating alone.

GAY. Who with?

LINDA. Pym Lovell.

GAY. (*Sits up abruptly and swings his feet to the floor.*) My God!

LINDA. I like Pym. He's a nice boy.

GAY. When you first meet Pym Lovell you think what a precocious boy until you meet his father, then you realize it's his father who's precocious. Why don't you have dinner with his father and have done with it?

LINDA. (*Smiles.*) Because his father's in London. Dine with us.

GAY. No, thanks. I'll stick around here.

LINDA. I'd cancel it, only he's broken a date for me.

GAY. (*Rises.*) I'll stay in and gather my thoughts. (*Moves around below desk toward the windows.*) Both of them. (*Laughs wryly.*) Ha, ha! (*Looks out the window.*)

LINDA. (*After a moment.*) I'll be back early.

GAY. No need for that. (*A silence.*)

LINDA. (*Not looking at him.*) Are we washed up, darling? (*Another pause.*)

GAY. (*With his back to her.*) What—?

LINDA. Are we washed up?

GAY. (*After a moment, turns and moves down to behind lower end of desk.*) Please, darling, don't let's go into the fundamentals tonight. I'm in no mood for it.

LINDA. O.K.! No fundamentals.

GAY. (*Feels he is being arbitrary and is irritated that she should make him feel arbitrary. Another pause while he moves to below lower end of desk.*) Every marriage goes through the doldrums sooner or later. We're in for ours. You've got to sit tight till we're through it.

LINDA. All right, dear.

GAY. Well, you ought to know that by this time.

LINDA. All right, dear.

GAY. (*Brutally.*) I love you.

LINDA. (*Sweetly.*) Thank you, dear.

GAY. Besides which, you know when I'm not working it's . . .

LINDA. (*Breaks in.*) I know. It's quite all right, dear. I'll keep out of your way.

GAY. (*Really irritated now.*) Darling, please don't be self-effacing! It doesn't become you. It's—

LINDA. (*Quickly.*) What would you like me to be?

GAY. (*In utter misery.*) Oh, for God's sake!

LINDA. (*Consciously goading him.*) Well, what?

GAY. Well, a little less all-seeing, a little less all-wise, a little less clairvoyant. (*Goes above desk to center, between chair and left lounge.*)

LINDA. (*Calmly.*) I am right then in assuming we're washed up.

GAY. (*Coldly.*) Sometimes by prophesying you make the undesirable come true.

LINDA. Not quite. No—I should want a little help from the outside. I imagine I'm getting it. (*Picks up a section of the newspaper and glances at it.*)

GAY. (*A pause. GAY turns slowly and moves a few steps toward her. Lightly.*) And—what—is behind that dark innuendo?

LINDA. (*Throws paper on desk and looks at him.*) A: You come home cold sober. B: Your abrupt concern over cosmic misery makes me guess you have one less cosmic.

GAY. (*This really makes him furious. Ominously.*) Oh, it does!

LINDA. (*Sweetly.*) I'm afraid so.

GAY. (*Pulls the center chair around to face opposite her and sits. Inarticulate with anger.*) Then let me tell you this:—my abrupt concern for cosmic misery as you so airily refer to the horrors of life pressing in daily and all around us—miseries not cosmic at all but extremely earthly—

LINDA. (*Quickly, unable to resist.*) Abrupt concern in your subject! Stick to it!

GAY. (*Furious at accepting help from the enemy, nevertheless accepting it.*) Well, may I tell you that my concern is not abrupt at all—not in the least abrupt. I've had it for some time—though you wouldn't suspect it from watching the—vehicles—I've manufactured so glibly for you to ride to success in. (*Pauses a moment, then slaps his knee with his hand.*) It's arrogant of you to take it for granted that since you are too complacent to be tortured by this concern that such complacence must be universal! (*Jumps up and paces over to below right lounge.*) If there's anything profoundly irritating it's the assumption that every general indignation may be traced to a private grievance. (*Turns to her.*) It must be true that women have capacity to absorb the abstract.

LINDA. (*Laughs, then reclines on sofa.*) I can absorb the particular—and I'd very much like to know who she is—this Miss Cosmos. (*Looks at GAY.*) Or Mrs. Perhaps Mrs. Cosmos? (*The house telephone on desk rings.* GAY *sits on the right lounge.* LINDA *reaches over back of sofa and picks up the receiver. Into receiver.*) Yes— No. I'll be right down. Thank you. (*Replaces the receiver.*) You know, darling, if only you got busy and wrote me a play matinee days. (*Reaches over back of sofa, picks up her hat on the desk, then rises and goes over to the mirror on down left wall and puts on the hat.*) We're much happier when I'm working. Haven't you noticed it? You know, when we're both idle it's kind of— (*Turns to him to display her hat.*) Like it?

GAY. (*Automatically, not looking really.*) Very much.

LINDA. Well, don't be overcome. (*Faces the mirror again for a final inspection, then goes to behind desk and picks up her gloves and bag.*) Sure you won't join us?

GAY. Quite.

LINDA. (*Moves around above desk up toward door.*) Good-bye, darling!

GAY. Have a good time.

HERE COME THE CLOWNS [1]

by

PHILIP BARRY

CLANCY, *a stagehand, has had all the hard-luck a man can bear. He is deeply troubled and seeks a meaning of life.* CONNIE *is a vibrant person. She loves* CLANCY. *She is trying to keep him out of the bar of Ma Speedy's Café, so he will not meet the wife who broke his heart.*

CONNIE. Do something for me?

CLANCY. What?

CONNIE. Will you promise to do it?

CLANCY. I will if I can.

CONNIE. You'll really promise?

CLANCY. If I—

CONNIE. No "ifs"!

CLANCY. Then I will.

CONNIE. Come up to the hall and dance a dance with me!

CLANCY. Oh no, Connie—what are you talking about?

CONNIE. You promised.

CLANCY. But I've forgotten how. My feet wouldn't—

CONNIE. You've not! It's not a thing, once known, you forget. It's like swimming or riding a bike—it stays with you. (*She holds out both hands to him.*) Come on—one dance, like in the old days.

CLANCY. God help me, I'll try. (*She snatches a white carna-*

---

[1] Copyright, 1937, 1939, by Philip Barry. Reprinted by permission of Coward-McCann, Inc.

tion from the vase on the table, breaks the stem and fixes the flower in his lapel.)

CONNIE. There! Now you look more like your old jaunty self! (CLANCY *gazes down at the flower.*)

CLANCY. That's an odd thing. He always used to wear one, didn't he?

CONNIE. Who did?

CLANCY. A man I know. (*Then his eyes look off into the far distance, across years, across water.*) Carnations—my father used to raise them in the gardens of Roche's Hotel in Glengariff, where he worked. And my mother told me once the white one was the flower of God, God bless her. And we had a lemon tree, too. They grow there, you know. There's a warm current passes the coast. Figs, as well—even a palm now and then. My, how that lemon tree used to smell of a morning! It was glorious. It was like heaven. (*He stops and passes hand over his face.*)—And still I was always wanting to go to Connemara. I never got there, I don't know why. The good Lord willed it otherwise, I suppose.

CONNIE. It was your father who wore the carnations?

CLANCY. No. Never him. They were too dear, and must be kept for the table. But a man I know did—and you know him, too. (*A moment's silence. Then* CONNIE *laughs lightly and slips her arm through his.*)

CONNIE. You and your lemon tree and carnations! Come along—you're day-dreaming! (*She leads him to the stairway.*) Just remember one thing, dancing—they don't whirl about as they did. (*They mount the stairs.*)

CLANCY. What is it they do, then?

CONNIE. You'll see! It always came natural to you, Dan! Once on the floor, you were like a man inspired.

CLANCY. Me grandfather claimed he introduced the waltz into Ireland. (*They are moving along the balcony now.*)

CONNIE. (*Mocking him.*)—Me grandmother claimed she introduced Irish to your grandfather.

CLANCY. The language or the whisky?

CONNIE. Both!—Will you promise to whirl me, Dan?

CLANCY. That I will—like a top on a table!

FOR THREE WOMEN

A FULL HOUSE [1]

by

FRED JACKSON

At the apartment that OTTILY *has rented on the fashionable side of town,* AUNTIE *and* DAPHNE *arrive from Yonkers, fearing the worst.*

OTTILY. (*To sofa, sits.*) Never mind her, tell me what brought you here, Auntie?

AUNTIE. (*To right of desk, sits.*) Well, if you want the truth, I've been worried sick about you.

OTTILY. About me? Why?

AUNTIE. For many reasons! I never slept a wink on your wedding night.

OTTILY. Why, Auntie, what kept you awake?

AUNTIE. I was uneasy. I couldn't help it. Your husband may be all right, my dear. I've no proof that he's not.

OTTILY. Why, Auntie, what do you mean?

AUNTIE. Remember, Ottily, you only knew this man two weeks before you married him! Think of it! Two weeks!

OTTILY. You can learn a lot of things in two weeks.

AUNTIE. Yes! That's why I'm still single!

DAPHNE. Goodness, Auntie, single all these years! What an awful time you've had getting acquainted with men!

AUNTIE. Daphne!

OTTILY. Well, I have George, that's all I care to know.

AUNTIE. Suppose he had another wife somewhere.

OTTILY. Oh, Auntie, how ridiculous!

AUNTIE. Or suppose he took fits?

OTTILY and DAPHNE. Fits, Auntie?

AUNTIE (*Circles above desk to* OTTILY *center.*) Fits! My cousin Sallie in Mount Kisco married a man she'd known a month —a handsome fellow—a real estate man! He was just as gentlemanly as anyone you ever saw. You couldn't see a thing wrong with him! But three days after the wedding he took a fit and chased her out into the hall of the hotel with nothing on but a bathrobe.

DAPHNE. How terrible if she'd met anybody she knew! (*At end of sofa.*) Yes, they might have recognized her.

OTTILY. George would never do anything like that. It's perfectly ridiculous of you to think of such things.

AUNTIE. (*Embracing her.*) I can't help it! After all, I brought you up. You're just the same as my own child and I'm worried about your living here with a perfect stranger!

OTTILY. Stranger! But he's my husband, Auntie!

AUNTIE. Even so!

OTTILY. He was meant to be my husband! We fell in love with each other at first sight and neither of us had ever looked at anyone else. It was Destiny made me marry him. It was Fate that brought him to Yonkers.

DAPHNE. Coming to Yonkers isn't Fate. It's a calamity. (*Sits on sofa.*)

AUNTIE. (*Goes to right, sits on bench.*) I told Daphne I could not draw another easy breath until I had been here to see for myself that you were all right!

DAPHNE. (*Rises, to* OTTILY.) You are all right, aren't you?

OTTILY. (*Center.*) You can't imagine how wildly, madly, gloriously happy I am—or rather—how happy I was—

DAPHNE. (*Left center.*) Was?

OTTILY. (*Center.*) Until George went away!

AUNTIE. (*Goes to her, right center.*) What?

DAPHNE. (*Left center.*) George—went—away?

OTTILY. (*Center, to* DAPHNE.) He—he—had to go—on—on—Wednesday!

AUNTIE. (*Right center.*) The day after your wedding?

DAPHNE. (*Left center.*) Why, what do you mean?

AUNTIE. (*Right center.*) Your husband deserted you the day after your wedding?

OTTILY. (*Center, to* AUNTIE.) Don't say deserted, Auntie. He was called away to Cleveland on business.

AUNTIE. (*Crowding* OTTILY *left a little.*) George Howell went off on a business trip the day after your wedding?

OTTILY. Yes.

AUNTIE. (*To right center a step.*) There's something wrong about that man!

OTTILY. (*Follows.*) But I told him to go! It meant money, and when you are married, you've got to think of such things!

AUNTIE. (*Turns to her.*) I suppose that's what he told you?

OTTILY. (*Hesitates.*) Yes.

AUNTIE. (*Right center.*) And what was this important business, I should like to know?

OTTILY. (*Center.*) It was something concerning a client. (*Goes left and turns.*) He couldn't reveal it to anyone! (*Goes left.*)

AUNTIE. (*Follows a step.*) Not even to you, his wife?

OTTILY. That's what he said.

AUNTIE. (*To right of desk.*) Daphne, I don't like the look of this at all. Not at all! He hasn't acted as if he were very glad to be with you!

DAPHNE. (*Goes left.*) I should think he would have made any sacrifice to have his honeymoon in peace! (OTTILY *is alone center.*)

OTTILY. (*To left of desk.*) But we are going to be together all the rest of our lives and—and he was only going to be gone for two days!

AUNTIE. (*Leaning over desk—right of it.*) Two days? But he's been away four already!

OTTILY. (*Left of desk.*) He intended to come back last night. I'll surely hear from him to-day. (*Goes center.*)

AUNTIE. (*Circles below desk to* OTTILY *center.*) You haven't even heard from him since he's been away?

OTTILY. (*Center.*) N-n-no, not—y-yet!

DAPHNE. (*To* OTTILY, *left center.*) Well, that is rather strange!

OTTILY. (*Center.*) No. He told me he wouldn't be able to write.

AUNTIE. Ha!

OTTILY. For business reasons.

AUNTIE. (*Right center.*) Well, isn't he friendly with the Western Union?

DAPHNE. (*Left center.*) How do you know he even went to Cleveland?

AUNTIE. (*Crowding* OTTILY *left a little.*) Did you see his ticket?

OTTILY. (*Just left of center.*) Of course not.

AUNTIE. (*Center.*) Cleveland! (*Jumping up.*) I just remembered. Where is that paper I brought in with me? (*Crosses right to desk.* DAPHNE *crosses quickly front of* OTTILY *to* AUNT.)

OTTILY. (*Center.*) What's the matter, Auntie? . . .

DAPHNE. (*Right center.*) The paper.

AUNTIE. (*At desk right of* DAPHNE.) There was something in it about an awful wreck somewhere. . . . (*She takes paper from desk.*) I've got it. Yes—here it is. Boston Flier Wrecked Near Hartford.

OTTILY. (*Sinks on sofa.* AUNT *drops paper center.* AUNT *and* DAPHNE *rush to comfort her.* AUNT *sits above her,* DAPHNE *below her on sofa.*) Oh, I knew it! I dreamed it!

AUNTIE. Perhaps it's for the best, my dear.

THE WARRIOR'S HUSBAND [1]

by

JULIAN THOMPSON

In the land of the Amazon Women, HIPPOLYTA *is Queen. She is regally handsome and brave.* ANTIOPE *is her spirited*

[1] Copyright, 1931, 1932, by Julian Thompson.

young sister. POMPOSIA *is the shrewd politician of the Amazons.*

HIPPOLYTA. Report your companies. (*To* BURIA.) Mobilize the entire Amazon army, ready to march at once. Have each company report as it falls in. Tell the Euxine light horse to mount. Their supplies can follow. Order my horse—and field equipment. (BURIA *crosses up steps and exits right two.*)

ANTIOPE. And mine too, Buria. Can't get along without the old gray mare. Thank the Gods, we've at last got someone to fight!

HIPPOLYTA. (*Coming down to stage level.*) An army of five thousand men! Why, it's a shame to put five thousand women up against them.

POMPOSIA. (*Right center, quickly.*) You haven't got five thousand under arms.

HIPPOLYTA. (*Left center, stops dead in her tracks.*) Well, you have equipment for the other two thousand that aren't equipped, haven't you?

POMPOSIA. Yes, but what are you going to use for money? I have to pay my artisans, you know.

ANTIOPE. (*Center.*) But, Pomposia—we've got to have that equipment. This is an emergency. You've got to make us a loan of it, or something.

HIPPOLYTA. Of course, Pomposia'll make a loan.

POMPOSIA. (*After a smiling pause.*) A loan? No—this is indeed a time of emergency, and I am prepared to do my part. It shall be a gift.

HIPPOLYTA. (*Enthused.*) A gift?

ANTIOPE. Good for you, Pomposia.

POMPOSIA. And I should like to call it a wedding gift.

HIPPOLYTA. A wedding gift?

POMPOSIA. It just occurred to me that, if you should make Sapiens your consort, I would give the equipment as a wedding gift.

ANTIOPE. What!

HIPPOLYTA. So that's your price, is it?

POMPOSIA. Oh, I didn't mean it that way, Your Majesty.

ANTIOPE. Don't do it, Hippolyta.

POMPOSIA. (*Stops center.*) In a national emergency of this kind I would be the last to stand in the way of our warriors having equipment.

HIPPOLYTA. (*Watching her.*) Of course you would.

POMPOSIA. Our people can not stand additional taxation. There are complaints as it is.

HIPPOLYTA. I know, I know.

POMPOSIA. And, so, if I throw my entire personal fortune into the defense to uphold your dynasty, wouldn't it be fair to let my family share in the dynasty?

ANTIOPE. (*To* HIPPOLYTA.) We can beat them with three thousand, Hippolyta, really we can.

POMPOSIA. And there are certain rather hostile elements in the realm which would be greatly pleased by such a wedding.

HIPPOLYTA. (*After a pause.*) All right—it's agreed, if I get the equipment.

POMPOSIA. You'll marry my Sappy.

HIPPOLYTA. Yes, I'll do anything to him you suggest. How do I marry him?

POMPOSIA. Why, you—you have to have a wedding ceremony.

HIPPOLYTA. What's that?

POMPOSIA. Well, as I understand it, you have to get a priestess or a notary public or something, and you and Sapiens swear before her.

ANTIOPE. What do they swear about?

POMPOSIA. They don't swear about anything. They each take an oath that they will be husband and wife.

ANTIOPE. And do they have to take her word for it?

HIPPOLYTA. (*To* POMPOSIA.) Get Heroica—(*Indicates her.*)—to swear us.

HEROICA. But, Your Majesty!

HIPPOLYTA. She swears in the warriors. Tell your son to prepare—and draw up the order to deliver the equipment to me

at once. Give it, Buria. When it is delivered we will complete
the marriage.

POMPOSIA. (*Going off right two.*) At once, Your Majesty, at
once.

ANTIOPE. (*To* HIPPOLYTA.) Well, are you completely crazy?
Do you mean to say you are going to marry that worm?

HIPPOLYTA. I've got to get that equipment. I can't risk three
thousand against five, even if they are men.

ANTIOPE. I know—but to marry that insect at all. . . .

HIPPOLYTA. Listen, Antiope. I'll get the equipment and marry
him. Then the equipment and I leave for the front. When we
get back will be time enough to decide what to do with him
and his mama.

ANTIOPE. I see.

FAMILY PORTRAIT [1]

by

LENORE COFFEE AND WILLIAM JOYCE COWEN

In an upper room in NATHAN's *house,* MARY *awaits Jesus'
return from Gethsemane. When the rest of the family jeered,*
MARY CLEOPHAS *stood by her, even taking the long journey to
Jerusalem.* MARY MAGDALEN *understands the seriousness of
the people's rising hatred against him.*

MARY. (*Enters down right, relieved at having sent the mes-
sage. Crosses below table to right of stool.*) Well, the little
boy has gone to tell him that we're here. I do feel better—

MARY CLEOPHAS. (*Around left of table to left of stool.*) That's
good! Now perhaps you'll sit down and rest yourself. (*Puts
her arm around* MARY *and sits her on stool. To* MAGDALEN.)
She's been on her feet the whole day—and we're neither of
us getting any younger.

MAGDALEN. (*To* MARY—*crossing right of table to below right stool.*) Is this your first visit to Jerusalem?

MARY. Oh dear, no, I came quite often as a girl. And then when my children grew up, I came with them. I've even been to Egypt!

MAGDALEN. Really? (MARY CLEOPHAS *crosses to chair left; sits.*) I've never travelled that far.

MARY. I didn't care much for it. But my husband—he was a carpenter—he got a lot of building ideas. (*Pause.*) If you're not too busy, I wish you'd stay and tell me about my son. I'm so hungry for first hand news of him.

MAGDALEN. (*To right of* MARY.) I'd love to.

MARY CLEOPHAS. We hear such mixed-up stories back home. He says one thing here in Jerusalem and by the time it's repeated all the way to Nazareth—well, you can imagine how it sounds! So she just had to come and find out for herself.

MARY. I've always tried to think of my other children—to see their side of it. Suddenly I couldn't any longer— It was as if they all just melted away. I didn't have any other children— Only this one—and he was in trouble.

MAGDALEN. (*Turns to get stool right of table—sees cloak.*) Oh, he's left his cloak! (*Takes cloak—looks off right, holding it.*)

MARY. (*Holding out her hand for cloak—*MAGDALEN *gives it to her.*) Isn't that just like him? Never thinks of himself. But I don't see why some of those disciples can't think of him once in a while. (*She cradles it in her arms.*)

MARY CLEOPHAS. Oh, they're too busy worrying about themselves! Who'll sit at the right hand and who'll sit at the left! So he goes out in the cold without a cloak! Just let something go wrong— When you get into trouble you find out who your friends are!

MAGDALEN. He knows that. That's what makes him so wonderful.

MARY. (*Surveying cloak.*) And it's torn, too! If I had a little thread I could mend it while I was waiting—

MAGDALEN. Leah usually keeps some up here. (*She looks around.*) Oh, I know—it's in the next room. (*She exits up right.*)

MARY CLEOPHAS. (*Rises—crosses to left of MARY.*) Mary, I think we ought to go home—back to Nazareth, I mean—

MARY. Without seeing him!

MARY CLEOPHAS. Well—no—but as soon as you do—

MARY. Oh, once I've seen him I'll do whatever he says.

MARY CLEOPHAS. This is no place for us to be.

MARY. But you were the one who didn't want to go any further—

MARY CLEOPHAS. Well, I feel differently now.

MARY. (*Gestures towards right too.*) Not because of her?

MARY CLEOPHAS. No. She's a real nice woman. You'd never think she'd led that kind of life.

MARY. S-sh—she'll hear you!

MARY CLEOPHAS. There must be something to the thing he teaches—to change a person that way.

MAGDALEN. (*Returning with needle and thread.*) Will this do?

MARY. Oh, thank you— (*Taking it.*) Yes—it's good and strong.

MAGDALEN. (*Moving left candelabra close to MARY.*) There, I think you'll have enough light.

MARY. (*Starts to sew. Looks up with smile.*) How this takes me back! When he was a little boy his knees went through everything! He played so hard. (MARY CLEOPHAS *sits down left in chair.*) And when he grew up and went into the carpenter shop he worked the same way. Never knew when it was time to stop.

MAGDALEN. (*Gets right stool—moves it right of MARY—sits.*) He's like that now. Works until he drops. He has so much he wants to say—he seems almost afraid he won't have time to say it. (*She quickly covers this ominous note by adding.*) The other day while he was talking it grew dark without his even knowing—and the people stayed on and listened—way into the night.

MARY CLEOPHAS. He always was a good talker. It's a real gift. (*Yawns.*)

MARY. What did he talk about that time?

MAGDALEN. About a shepherd who lost one sheep. And how he left the whole flock and searched and searched the night through until he found it. And how happy it made him and what it meant to him to bring that one lost sheep back into the fold. I love that story.